AF265903

Endorsements

Postcards from H♥ME has resonated with readers, educators, and professionals who believe in the importance of meaningful communication and connection. Their reflections highlight the value of small acts of encouragement and the lasting impact that thoughtful words can have on the lives of others.

Postcards from H♥ME Endorsements

"Postcards from H♥ME provides a special way to connect versus just communicate with your loved ones. The act of handwriting and receiving a physical message creates a unique bond. Reading this book will be inspirational and fun. Kudos to Sandy!"

Susan Law Dake

"Insightful and inspiring, Postcards from H♥ME is a beautiful reminder of the true power of putting pen to paper. In a world dominated by quick texts and fleeting messages, this book rekindles the timeless magic of handwritten words, capturing memories, emotions, and connections in a way that feels both personal and enduring. A heartfelt tribute to the art of meaningful communication, Postcards from H♥ME will leave readers reflecting on the simple yet profound act of sharing a piece of themselves through the written word."

Barbara Jean Sellick

"The daily postcards I received during my undergraduate years at Notre Dame strengthened my transition to independence while living over 700 miles from home. They reminded me that no matter the distance, I always had family to rely on. Thanks, Mom."

Tanner Tarkleson
Son and Recipient of the Daily Postcards

"I have watched Sandra live the message of this book long before she ever wrote it. I stood beside her during some of the most difficult seasons of her life and saw firsthand how she chose love, consistency, and presence even when it would have been easier to retreat. Throughout her children's college years, she proved that connection does not disappear with distance. Postcards from H♥ME is not simply a story about motherhood. It is a reminder that small, intentional acts create emotional security and lasting bonds in a world that feels increasingly disconnected. I am grateful for our continued friendship and for the steady example she sets every single day."

Kelly Esposito
Friend and witness to the journey

"My Mom is one of the most amazing people I know.
My Mom loves like no one else in the world. My Mom knows when I'm sad before I do. My Mom is strong and passionate.
My Mom makes everyday things special.
My Mom sent me a postcard every day for four years. I looked forward to every single one.
If you don't believe in the power of the written word, take it from a college kid who looked forward to going to the mailroom every week, a small note means so much more than you can imagine. Read "Postcards from H♥ME" for an in-depth look at how postcards brought us closer than ever.
Mom, I am so proud of you. I love you so much."

Kallie Tarkleson ♥
Daughter and Recipient of the Daily Postcards

"As a health educator, I see firsthand how important consistent support is for young adults navigating stress and transition. Postcards from H♥ME beautifully illustrates how small, intentional acts of connection can strengthen resilience and emotional well-being."

Holly Louis
Health Educator, Saratoga Springs High School

"Working closely with Sandra, I've had the opportunity to see the thoughtfulness and authenticity she brings to every relationship. She genuinely cares about the people she works with and, is intentional in everything she does. Postcards from H♥ME reflects that same sincerity and serves as a meaningful reminder that true connection doesn't happen by chance it's created with purpose."

Angela Fedullo

"Postcards from H♥ME is a beautiful reminder that meaningful connection doesn't require a screen, just a thoughtful message and a moment of intention. In a world dominated by texts and emails, this book inspires us to rediscover the joy of sending something tangible, personal, and lasting. It is a heartfelt and timely invitation to reconnect in the most human way."

Heather L. Rooney

"Throughout the 18 years that I have worked in Central Mail Services, I have undoubtedly sorted through thousands of pieces of mail. I can tell you that nothing brings a bigger smile to a student's face like a piece of mail from home. Students who are blessed to receive those handwritten messages have that extra piece of support I wish we could give all the students. Postcards from H♥ME reflects the importance of that needed connection (on both ends) as young adults are navigating their way from the comfort of home and into the world they are preparing to conquer."

Laura Sullivan

Central Mail Services, Supervisor Nazareth University

"One of the hallmarks of the Notre Dame community is the belief that faith, friendship, and encouragement should accompany students long after they leave campus. Postcards from H♥ME captures that spirit beautifully, demonstrating how thoughtful, consistent communication can provide strength and connection during life's transitions."

Dan Hulihan
President, Notre Dame Club of Northeastern New York

"I've watched Sandy pour her heart into this book, and that love and care shine through on every page. As a newer mother myself, Postcards from H♥ME stirred emotions I didn't expect and reminded me how powerful the small acts of love and connection between parent and child can be. Sandy's tradition of sending daily postcards to her children is a beautiful reminder that even the simplest gestures can carry love across any distance. Honest, heartfelt, and inspiring, this story will leave you reflecting on the moments that matter most and holding them a little tighter."

Casey Castiglione

"The digital world has caused us to lose the art of communication. Not many people take the time to express their thoughts and feelings in a meaningful way. With Postcards from H♥ME, Sandy has reiterated the importance of family, communication and feelings. This book allows us to be part of her life as she migrated through her emotions. We get to share these monumental moments with her and immerse ourselves into the feelings of joy she brought to the masses."

John Constantino
CEO/Publisher

LETTERS FROM MY CHILDREN

"I don't remember the first few postcards arriving, likely because it wasn't unusual in our family to receive one from a trip that someone else took. Eventually, the pace increased and I began to wonder if this was going to be a daily occurrence. When they did, picking them up became part of my afternoon routine.

Adjusting to life away from home was more difficult than I anticipated, and these postcards served as a reminder that I had at least some semblance of a safety net despite being many miles from home. My time spent reading the words was constrained within the two-minute walk from the mailbox to my dorm room. After some time, however, it became less about what they said than the fact that they arrived. I knew that there was intention behind it. This support fueled me in ways I can only see through a retrospective lens.

While it's difficult to remember the moment-to-moment events that were eased by the knowledge that someone cared so deeply, I know that it pushed me through the most difficult times. Friends and mailroom staff came to comment on the weekly influx of postcards in a way that transitioned from half-sarcasm to an inspired tone. As mentioned in this book, there would even be disappointment from others on the occasional missed day.

Now, I look at the collection of postcards that I've amassed with an appreciation for the little gestures in life. I'm gifted with the knowledge that consistency, rather than elaborate gestures, is part of the recipe for meaningful relationships."

Tanner Tarkleson,
Son and Recipient of the Daily Postcards

If you picked up this book by chance, you are very lucky.

Is there anyone in your life you miss? Is there anyone you wish you were closer to? Is there something you need to say, but you don't know how to say it? Then let's start here, within the pages of "Postcards from H♥ME."

When I left for college, I thought I would be able to call my mom to stay in touch. But as my freshman year went on, classes and jobs got serious. I quickly became overwhelmed with class work, studying, and making friends that calling home became a rare occurrence. I would call my mom briefly, a quick "hi" while walking between classes, or "Mom, I'm stressed and I'm tired" on the way back to the dorm. But there was only so much energy I could give on those phone calls. I missed my mom.

In those first weeks of school, I got an email from my college mail room, "You have received a letter." For some reason, that message sparked so much joy in me that I dropped everything and ran to the mail room to pick up my first postcard from home. The postcards never said much; they're small, but somehow Mom always knew what I needed to hear. And they always arrived at the right time. I remember I had a week where I was really struggling and never told my Mom. That next week I picked up a stack of postcards and one of them read,

"Everything will be alright. I love you and I'm proud of you. M♥M." That little message had me crying on my twin xl mattress. From so far away, my mom knew I needed extra support. Something about the words on the postcard struck me harder than a text would have. Seeing my mothers handwriting telling me she's proud of me at the time I needed it most, meant the world to me. It kept me going. It lit a fire underneath me. "I can do this" I thought.

If you are thinking about someone, write them a letter. If you miss someone, write them a postcard and tell them why. There is something magical that happens when you take the time to hand write something in this age where everything is instantaneous. Handwriting shows others that you care, that you have time.

Kallie Ann Tarkleson

Daughter and Recipient of the Daily Postcards

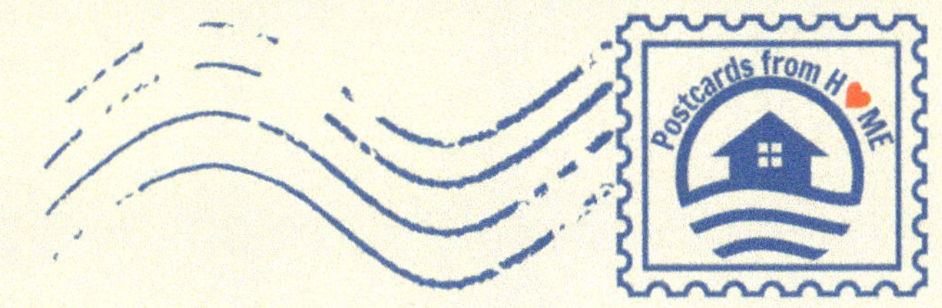

POSTCARDS FROM HOME

Close at Heart. Miles Apart

For Parents Through Change and Distance

SANDRA TARKLESON

Postcards from H♥ME
Close at Heart. Miles Apart
For Parents Through Change and Distance

ISBN: 978-1-965761-90-8 (Hardcover)
ISBN: 978-1-965761-92-2 (Paperback)
ISBN: 978-1-965761-91-5 (eBook)
Library of Congress Control Number: 2026906065

Published by Spotlight Publishing House™
Goodyear, AZ 85338
www.spotlightpublishinghouse.com

Editor: Susan Crossman
www.crossmancommunications.com
Cover Design: Sandra Tarkleson
www.postcardsfromhome.net

Disclaimer

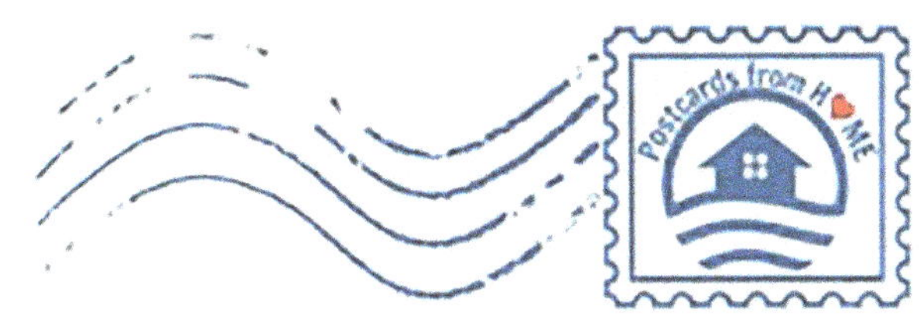

This book details the author's personal opinions, and she makes no representations or warranties of any kind with respect to this book or its contents. The statements made in this book are not intended to diagnose, treat, cure, or prevent any condition or unhappiness. They are meant to assist you in navigating your life and do not replace medical care or therapy.

All content is for informational and educational purposes and does not establish any kind of patient/client relationship. The information presented here is not a substitute for any kind of professional advice. Please consult with your own therapist or other healthcare specialist regarding the suggestions and recommendations made in this book. Before you begin any program, or change your lifestyle in any way, you should consult your physician or another licensed practitioner to ensure that you are in good health and that the examples contained in this book will not harm you.

Except as specifically stated in this book, neither the author, the editor, nor the publisher, nor any authors, contributors, or other representatives, will be liable for damages arising out of or in connection with the use of this book.

This is a comprehensive limitation of liability that applies to all damages of any kind, including (without limitation) compensatory; direct, indirect, or consequential damages; loss of data, income, or profit; loss of or damage to property and claims of third parties.

If you are experiencing severe anxiety and depression or an immediate crisis, please reach out to a mental health professional or crisis center or hotline.

Dedication

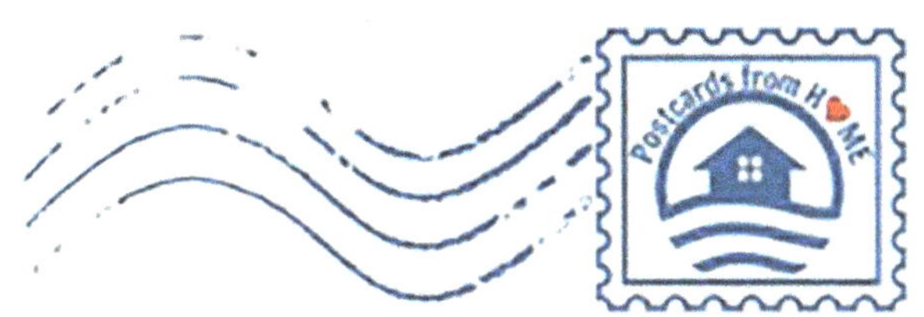

For Tanner and Kallie, *who gave me the best title in all the world: Mom. Every postcard was signed M♥M, and to this day, that is how I sign my love. This book exists because of my smart, talented, loving children who taught me that love travels any distance, that small acts create big changes, and that the greatest adventures begin when we choose connection over fear.*

For My Parents, Wayne and Mary Anne Duso, *who showed me what unwavering support looks like and who became the safety net my children needed when their world shifted beneath their feet.*

For Knute, *my Golden Retriever and faithful writing companion, who spent countless hours by my side at the computer when he would rather have been playing ball.*

For Kelly Esposito, *who continues to show me what true friendship is, day after day.*

For everyone still learning that we are all connected by invisible threads of love, one postcard at a time.

Contents

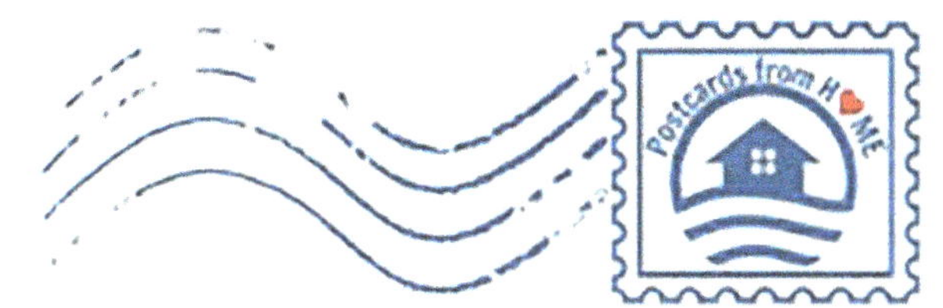

Chapter 1

The Card That Sparked a (R)evolution

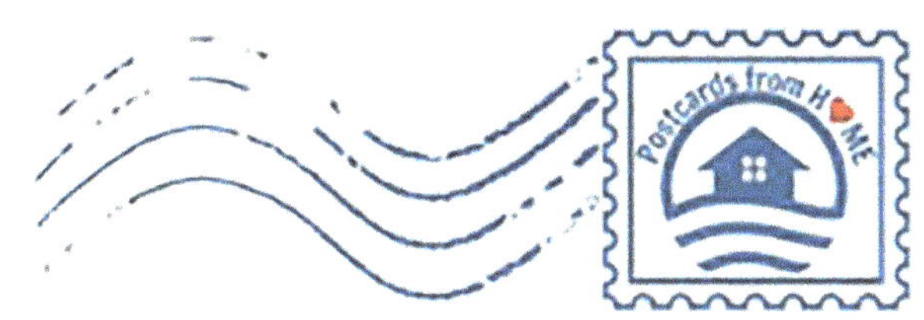

One year after my son Tanner graduated from the University of Notre Dame, we returned for a home game in South Bend, Indiana. The campus, in many ways, felt like home. We walked the grounds, visited his old dorm, Duncan Hall, and reflected on how quickly those four years had passed.

Before the game, we ran into his former dorm rector, and what he told me stopped me in my tracks. He said he missed seeing the daily postcards I had sent to Tanner. In all his years in that role, he had never witnessed anything like it. He described them as a piece of joy from home that brightened not only Tanner's day, but his as well.

That conversation happened years after what began as a simple way to stay connected had become something far greater than I ever expected, a practice that would touch lives I would never know in ways I never could have imagined.

Life is a series of choices made every day, every moment. Life, like a book, is filled with chapters. Some will make you cry; some will lock you in and capture all your attention; others will make you wonder about your own life, who you are, what you have become. Some chapters unravel your story so completely that it's hard to keep reading. Life and books have something in common: a beginning and an end.

We are born; we die. We start school and eventually graduate. We take jobs and hope to retire. We fall in love, get married, begin a family and, unfortunately, for roughly half of those families, experience divorce. Some beginnings are beautiful, some happen by chance or through divine intervention, and some are heartbreaking.

Yet life has a way of bringing us to where we were truly meant to be, or at least that is what I hope.

Usually, however, we go through life not thinking about the beginning or the ending, and as a result we, as a society, have become very "robotic." It's Tuesday, so we have tacos. On Monday we take out the trash or mow the lawn. We follow patterns and perform daily rituals.

We forget to look up. We busily text, scroll, and tap our phones to "like" a funny video while simultaneously missing what is right in front of us. If we are looking at our phones, social media, or something else to make ourselves feel better, we are looking in the wrong direction; it has been scientifically proven that when we look up, we feel better. The next time you feel discouraged, anxious, or stressed, look up and expand your focus. It can enhance your brain function and make you feel calmer.[1]

We also rush from task to task. Why? Ask yourself why you are rushing to work, hurrying to get somewhere. Relax. Enjoy the in-between moments you are rushing to get through. You may find what you need there.

My mother used to say, "It's not about what you eat. It's about who you eat it with." Over time, I realized that's true of everything in life. It's not about the postcard, the house, or the paycheck, or the perfectly orchestrated moment. It's about people. It's about connections. It is about being present. I have told my children on numerous occasions that God gives us a gift every day, it is called the present, what are you going to do with yours?

This book isn't just about my story. It's about the idea that small acts of love, the ones so many people overlook, are the ones that change everything. This book will also take you through the seasons that so many of us face after divorce, learning to survive one day at a time while carrying the added responsibility of raising children.

It's written with the intention of sharing the tools that took me years to discover, offering comfort and connection to parents who are struggling to stay grounded, to navigate solitude, and to face the bittersweet moment of watching their children leave home.

Every ripple begins somewhere, and mine begins with a single postcard.

How It All Started

My habit of sending postcards to my son after he left for college eventually became Postcards from H♥ME, both the name of this book and a practice that changed my life. It started as my way of staying connected. A small thread between home and the world Tanner was stepping into. Even though I was looking forward to spending meaningful one-on-one time with my daughter, Kallie, who was going into her junior year of high school, I also wanted Tanner to know he wasn't forgotten. I didn't want to hover. I didn't want to disappear. I wanted him to know that even as he moved into his own life, I would forever be on his side.

So, I began looking for something simple, something small, inexpensive, unremarkable, yet meaningful. That's when I found the postcard. A handful of words, a picture from home, and a little piece of love he could hold in his hands. What started as one postcard became a rhythm, a heartbeat, and a daily connection. Nearly every day of the school year, a piece of home landed in a college mailbox, a quiet reminder that love doesn't disappear with distance. And later, when Kallie went off to college, those same reminders found their way to her, too. Over time, those postcards became their own story, piled high on my kids' dorm room walls, tucked into shoeboxes, and carried in conversations.

The Ripple Effect: Why This Book Exists

Science now indicates what many of us have always known in our hearts: Small, intentional acts of connection can reshape lives.

Research from the HeartMath Institute demonstrates that heart centered emotions like gratitude, love, and compassion create measurable electromagnetic fields around our bodies, fields that are felt by others, even at a distance.[2]

Studies from Dr. James Pennebaker at the University of Texas show that expressive writing, just a few minutes a day, boosts mental health, strengthens emotional regulation, and even improves physical health outcomes.[3]

The Harvard Study of Adult Development, the longest longitudinal study ever conducted on human happiness, concludes simply: "The quality of our relationships determines the quality of our lives."[4]

Connection isn't a luxury. It's not a "nice to have." It's what makes life meaningful. And in a world that increasingly encourages distraction, comparison, and surface level interaction, choosing to show up for someone consistently and intentionally becomes a gift beyond measure.

Why Handwriting Still Matters

In an age where everything moves at the speed of a double tap or a swipe, handwriting matters more than ever. It forces us to slow down. It forces us to think about the person at the other end. It demands presence, not performance. Postcards don't have filters. It doesn't have algorithms. It has fingerprints. It has imperfections. It has a heart. And those qualities are what people crave, even if they don't realize it yet.

Handwritten words travel differently. They feel different. They are remembered differently. You may not remember a text you received last week, but you'll remember a postcard someone sent you when you needed to know you mattered.

Science says it. Our souls know it. Now we just need to rediscover it.

This Is More Than a Story

This book is intended to help you stop, pause, look around, be present, love who you are, and care deeply. It isn't my entire story; it's a collection of pieces that shaped me, the moments that taught me the most about love, distance, and presence. I didn't want to bore you with every detail of my life, but rather to share the parts that mattered, the ones that changed me and might help you see your own life a little differently.

It began as the story of how I stayed connected to my children as they left for college but, over time, those small moments of connection became much greater. They showed me how simple acts of care could ripple outward, touch others, and ultimately become my new mission, the foundation for everything I've built around Postcards from H♥ME.

It is my hope that through this book you will find yourself reflecting on your own journey and that it will inspire you to live with more intention, be more present, and love with your entire heart. And maybe, along the way, you'll feel inspired to reach for a pen and a postcard, a notecard, or something tangible, to remind someone or even yourself; that connection still matters.

I share how my family traditions were built without planning and how many of them became the glue we didn't even know we needed. This is my story of heartbreak, betrayal, and financial loss, told not through pretending to be perfect, but through showing up one small act at a time.

What began as a way to stay close to my children through postcards became something deeper, a reflection of how love can travel, how simple consistency can leave an imprint far beyond what we see. I didn't know then how far those small gestures would ripple or how they would eventually return to me as stories from others who had been touched by the idea. Those moments became this book.

At the end of this book, you'll be invited to discover for yourself what I've learned about the lost art of writing a simple postcard. And if, along the way, you feel inspired to share your own story, send a smile, or brighten someone's day, I welcome you to visit me at postcardsfromhome.net, where you can read new stories, gather ideas to keep you writing, and join a growing community devoted to rediscovering connection, one handwritten note at a time.

As I moved through this season of my life, I didn't realize the impact these small acts were having. Looking back now, I know they were more than gestures; they were lifelines.

Over time, what began as a simple practice of writing, sending, and connecting became more than a habit. It became my purpose.

This isn't about nostalgia. It's about hope in motion. It's about choosing a presence over performance. It's about healing the spaces between us, one simple, sacred, handwritten moment at a time.

---

1. "Horizon Gazing and Its Health Benefits," *Sensory Trust*, n.d., accessed November 21, 2025, https://www.sensorytrust.org.uk/blog/horizon-gazing-and-its-health-benefits/.
2. R. McCraty and D. Childre, "Coherence: Bridging Personal, Social, and Global Health," *Alternative Therapies in Health and Medicine* 16(4) (2010):10–24.
3. J. W. Pennebaker, *Opening Up: The Healing Power of Expressing Emotions* (New York: Guilford Press, 1997), 3–6.
4. R. J. Waldinger and M. S. Schulz, *The Good Life: Lessons from the World's Longest Scientific Study of Happiness* (New York: Simon & Schuster, 2023).

Chapter 2

The Day Everything Changed

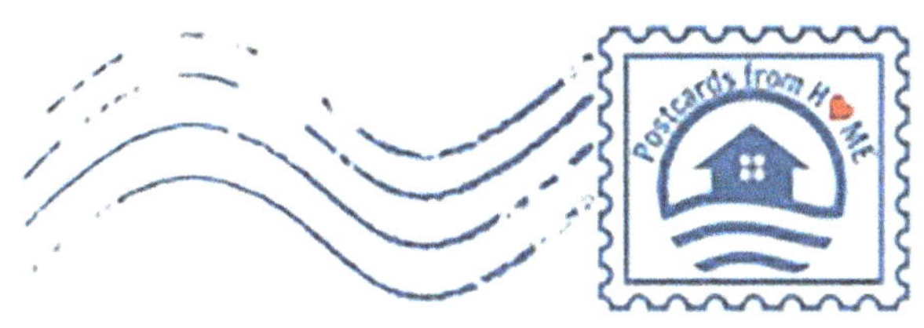

The acceptance email arrived at 1842 military time; the same year the University of Notre Dame was founded. I remember the day like it was yesterday. It was a gray and cold afternoon in March, the kind that makes it hard to believe spring will ever arrive, and the temperature still hovered near freezing. My son, Tanner, wanted to read the message alone in his room. I do not recall what time he went downstairs, but Kallie and I sat in the living room for what seemed like hours. The countdown felt endless. My thoughts spiraled: Would he get in? What if he did not? I prayed and then, as though a shockwave moved through the house, we heard:

"I GOT IN! I GOT IN!"

I felt excited, proud, and energized all at once. Notre Dame was eleven-and-a-half hours away by car, a lifetime away by heart.

Everything about that moment felt electric. We called family and friends, and one special call went to Meme and Pepe, Tanner's grandparents. Pepe was the ultimate ND fan; he had worn the same "Fighting Irish" jersey my entire childhood. It was dark blue with quarter-length sleeves and a large "91" in ND gold across the front. He had worn it so long it was patched in several places. We cried, laughed, and made a quick trip to the sporting goods store for anything covered with the Fighting Irish logo. That day felt like Christmas and the Fourth of July rolled into one.

Later that night, when the calls ended and the new ND sweatshirts were folded away, I sat alone in the kitchen with a truth I was not ready to face: My son was leaving.

The Space Between Hovering and Disappearing

Every parent who has experienced this knows this kind of heartbreak. It is not clean, like the end of a relationship or the loss of a job. It is messy and contradictory because it is exactly what you have been working toward for eighteen years, and it is also the thing that threatens to hollow you out completely.

I had spent nearly two decades teaching my son to be independent, to think for himself, to trust his judgment. I celebrated every milestone, his first drive to school, his first job, the evenings he went out without needing directions. I wanted him to be capable and confident, and ready for the world.

But I also wanted him to still need me, at least a little.

The fear of becoming a "hover mom" haunted me. I had seen it happen: the parents who could not let go, who called professors, who mediated roommate issues. I refused to be that person, but I also refused to disappear. There had to be something in between: a way to stay connected without clutching, to remain present without being intrusive. A way to remind my son that love does not have an expiration date or a distance limit. I just did not yet know what that looked like.

The Weight of Single Motherhood

This fear felt different from what my married friends described when they talked about their children leaving for college. They had partners or spouses to share both the grief and the joy, the excitement, worry, and bittersweet relief that come with letting go.

They had someone beside them to remind them that this was natural, healthy, and the goal they had been working toward all along.

I had Tanner's sister, still two years away from her own departure, and I had my parents, extended family, and dear friends who surrounded us with love. Yet the quiet inside my house still felt heavy.

My ex and I separated when the children were in middle school, and that season marked a significant shift in our family life. By the time we finalized our divorce in 2015, I had already been navigating much of their daily life on my own, and that period was hard for all of us. During that time, Tanner, Kallie, and I grew closer as we settled into a new rhythm together. We shared conversations about school, sports, friendships, musicals, shows, and the everyday moments that filled our days. I stayed up late when help was needed and spent countless hours in bleachers for basketball, volleyball, and tennis games, Tae Kwon Do tournaments and sitting in the audience for performances and shows. By the time Tanner left for college in 2017, we had become a close, newly shaped family. That chapter had already been formed by years of showing up for one another.

Not because his father was absent, but because everyday life happened with me.

I took that opportunity seriously, creating a home that felt anchored and warm: I lit candles at dinner, played music, served pancakes on Sundays, and celebrated laughter from the kitchen. I wanted my children to feel protected enough to grow and brave enough to leave.

The weight of single motherhood was heavy, but I wore it willingly.

The Months of Waiting

Spring turned to summer, and the reality of Tanner's departure became tangible. Everything came electronically, emails about orientation, checklists, and dorm information. The formal acceptance letter arrived later by mail. We made lists of what he would need and mapped the long drive to South Bend, Indiana.

I began paying attention to ordinary moments with new intensity. The way he spoke, the music he played, the jokes he shared with Kallie. I memorized his laugh, his energy, the sound of him singing Dear Theodosia from the play, *Hamilton*. One evening in July, I looked at him across the room and said quietly, "I am really going to miss having you around." He smiled in that half bashful way teenagers do when they pretend not to feel the same thing.

Those small exchanges, the rhythm of living together, were what I knew I would miss most, not the milestones but the little things, the easy familiarity that builds over time. That is what makes a house feel like home.

How do you prepare to lose that?

The Moment of Inspiration

The idea came on an ordinary afternoon, months after the acceptance email had arrived. I was scrolling online for last-minute dorm essentials when postcards appeared on my screen. Not just any postcards, Star Wars postcards. A boxed set of scenes and characters from the movies that had quietly framed Tanner's childhood.

I stopped scrolling. Star Wars had always held a special place in his world. He and his best friend had discovered the original trilogy together and had been hooked from the start. Weekend marathons, inside jokes, and lightsaber duels in the yard were their thing, a language of friendship.

Seeing those postcards sparked something in me. They felt like a bridge, a way to stay close without hovering, to send love and encouragement one scene at a time.

The images were simple: Luke Skywalker beneath twin suns, Princess Leia in white, Darth Vader's helmet, the Millennium Falcon in flight. Something about them felt right.

I remembered the letters I had received during my own college years. Back then, handwritten words were lifelines. And just like that, the answer was in front of me. I knew what I had to do.

I added the Star Wars postcards to my cart, then went back and bought three more sets: Where's Waldo? Funny Animals, and Fun Facts.

Practice Takes Shape

There were no plans. I just began sending postcards. Each card was a small extension of home, a few lines to let him know he was loved.

Before that first card ever arrived, we attended the Mass for incoming freshmen at the Joyce Center. Parents filled the arena; students sat below, and the music rose through the arena. When it ended, we met our children on the floor to say goodbye. I held my son tightly, trying to memorize the feeling of that moment. I was happy for him and knew he would thrive, but a piece of my heart stayed in South Bend that day. The tears came without warning.

I was grateful that my daughter was with me on the drive home. We talked about everything and nothing, about her remaining years of high school and what this new season meant for both of us. We promised that this would be our special time to create new memories before her own next chapter began. In that car, somewhere between Indiana and home, I realized those postcards would keep one connection alive while another was just beginning.

What Friends Said

I did not tell many people what I was doing. When friends saw the postcards or caught me writing one, they asked questions. Postcards are rare now; most people buy them as souvenirs, not to send.

"That is so sweet," some said, half teasing.

"Why would you do that?" others asked. "You could just call or text."

I understood. In an age of instant communication, postcards seemed unnecessary.

But they felt different. They did not demand a reply. They were quiet reminders that love endures.

My siblings remembered our mom sending postcards when we were in college. My sister, who had a son in college, thought it was a wonderful idea. Those little notes started conversations I had not expected about how connection looks different for everyone.

The Deeper Why

The postcards were for me, just as much as for my children. Writing gave me a way to process my emotions about Tanner leaving, as well as my daughter's eventual departure. Although my thoughts were rarely stated outright in what I wrote, the act itself became a place for them to live. I did not realize it at the time. That simple act became something quietly powerful.

Each morning (or whenever I could find a moment), coffee nearby, I would choose a postcard and write a few lines, sometimes a funny story, a memory, or an observation. Sometimes I would write them at home, sometimes at work, wherever I happened to be. I kept the postcards and stamps in a journal where I kept small notes about what was going on in Tanner's life, a habit that later inspired what I now share on my website. It became a practice of gratitude, a way to notice what was good instead of what was missing.

What I Did Not Know Then

When I sent that first postcard, I thought I was simply staying connected without intruding. I did not realize I was beginning something that would ripple outward.

I did not know Tanner's dorm rector would look forward to those cards, that postal workers would notice them, or that other parents would start their own traditions.

I did not know those small pieces of cardstock would become lifelines during the hardest college moments, reminders that my children were never alone.

I did not know that writing those cards, wherever I was, would teach me about presence and consistency and the quiet power of showing up in small ways.

All I knew initially was that my heart needed a way to travel across those eleven-and-a-half hours. In those first weeks, I dated each postcard to see how long it took to reach Tanner, so I could pause mailing before breaks and resume when he returned.

Somehow, between my kitchen table and his mailbox, I found a rhythm that felt like home.

The day everything changed was not the day Tanner got accepted to Notre Dame. It was the day I realized that love does not need permission from distance and that the smallest acts can carry the biggest truth.

It was the day I bought my first pack of postcards and chose connection over fear.

It was the day I learned that sometimes the most powerful thing you can do is simply show up, quietly and consistently, with love in your heart and a pen in your hand.

Chapter 3

Building Connection from the Ground Up

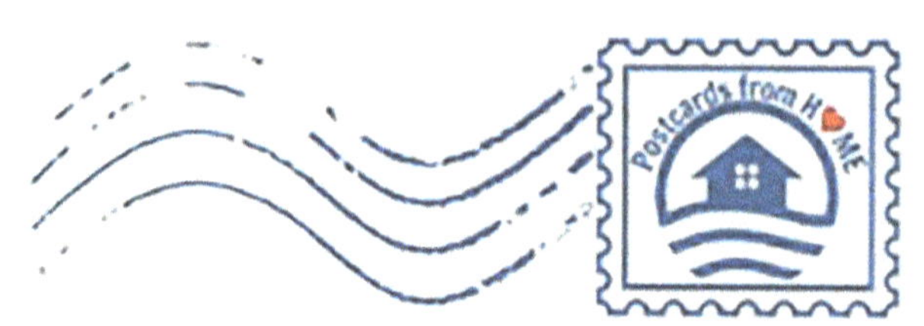

The day was warm, nearly ninety-five degrees, and the sun glared down as I stood by my mailbox. I could barely manage a thought outside the battle in my head that had been going on all day. The heat mimicked the guilt I was holding in. The air felt heavy against my skin as I tried to keep it all together.

I do not know what made me say it out loud that day. Maybe it was the sun.

Maybe it was silence. Or maybe it was the fact that I had just picked up the mail and could not hold one more thing, not even my own story. Near me stood a woman at her mailbox. We had never really spoken, maybe waved once or twice. But on that day, of all days, I opened my mouth and said, "My husband asked for a divorce."

Just like that. No context. No warning. No apology for oversharing. The words simply slipped out, as if they had been lodged in my throat for weeks, waiting for air. And here is the thing: She did not flinch. She did not look away. She did not gasp or shift uncomfortably. She nodded, as though she had heard that kind of truth before, as though she knew what it was to hold mail in one hand and grief in the other.

That was Kelly.

We did not know it then, but that single moment would begin a friendship that would hold us both up through some of the hardest years of our lives.

Learning What Connection Really Looks Like

When my marriage began to unravel, not much changed outwardly. By the time it officially ended in 2015, the truth had already been unfolding for years. The unraveling was slow and quiet, stretched across countless late nights of trying, forgiving, and pretending everything was fine. It wasn't one explosive moment. It was the slow fading of something that had once felt certain.

During those long in-between years, my children were still in grade school, old enough to sense the tension but young enough to need stability and reassurance. The house still hummed with routines and laughter, but underneath it all lived the quiet ache of change. Even when you have carried the weight alone, grief still finds its way in when the final thread breaks. It's not only the end of a marriage; it's the end of what you once hoped it could become, the end of the future you thought you were building together.

That was when Kelly appeared, almost as if sent by divine timing. We began walking together, sometimes in silence, sometimes pouring out the words we had both been holding in. We shared coffee, swapped stories, and occasionally sat with a glass of wine on the porch as the sky dimmed, just talking about everything and nothing. There was no need to pretend, no pressure to be fine.

We laughed, cried, and learned how to live again.

From the beginning, we made a quiet promise to each other: there would be no judgment, no expectations, no criteria to meet. We could show up exactly as we were.

We called it our tennis match of support: Sometimes it was her turn to serve, sometimes mine. She would text a simple "Need anything?" or leave a cup of coffee on my porch. I would listen when her day fell apart, or walk with her until the air cleared.

There were things we never shared beyond our circle, private moments that belonged only to our friendship. But what mattered most was the safety we found in each other's presence. The permission to be fully ourselves, even when those selves were tired, angry, or uncertain.

Kelly wasn't the only person who helped me through those years, but she was the one who most clearly mirrored my experience. Her understanding ran deep because she, too, was navigating her own loss. That shared pain and faith turned into something steady and sacred. She remains one of the most valuable people in my life. Our friendship is as authentic now as it was then, rooted in showing up without expectation, in loving each other exactly as we are.

In many ways, the lessons I learned beside Kelly would later echo through the postcards I wrote to my children: Connection happens in the quiet spaces where love simply shows up.

Building a Family from Scratch

The difficult years were just that, difficult. I could go on about the frustrations, the anger, the tangled emotions that came with them, but my story is not unique. It is the story of many divorced women learning how to hold themselves together while holding everything else, too.

One evening, after a long and exhausting day, I sat on the edge of my bed with tears running down my cheeks, and something became clear. I wasn't making a new promise. I was returning to one I had made long ago. I had already committed to pour every ounce of love I had into being my children's mother, into creating a home where they felt safe, seen, and celebrated, where their happiness was protected, even when mine had to wait.

There is no manual for keeping a family together when one person walks away, so I made one up. I wrote it with glue sticks and school forms, Tae Kwon Do uniforms and Target runs, with summer mornings that started with pancakes and ended with camp drop offs. I wrote it through drum lessons and packed lunches, bedtime stories and emergency room visits, science kits from the clearance aisle at Walmart. It was never about perfection; it was about presence.

I remember buying the next grade up in workbooks: If they were in first grade, we practiced second. Not because I was pushing them, but because I wanted them to feel capable, prepared, and proud. I wanted them to know they were smart, loved, and worth the time it took to sit beside them and solve a fraction problem on a summer afternoon.

We had a one-week-on, one-week-off arrangement with their father, a schedule that required constant transitions and never sat easily with the children. Over time, much of their daily life unfolded with me. During our marriage, I had always been a mom in the more traditional sense, the one who stayed home, cooked, cleaned, and cared for the children. It was a privilege, and I took being a mother seriously. It was not a burden to keep filling that role after the marriage ended; it was a calling. That became my family, the one I created in the middle of heartbreak, built from love, a handful of coupons, and an unshakable belief that this, too, shall pass.

Kelly was part of that foundation, the friend who reminded me I was doing better than I believed. She was there for birthdays, school concerts, and those small victories that no one else saw. But she was not alone in that support. I was blessed with other friends, some from college, some from work, others from my community, each offering something different but equally important. They were the ones who brought meals, who called at midnight just to check in, who made me laugh when I wanted to cry.

Through all of it, I realized I had something far greater than money or certainty. I had friends who loved me for me, who asked for nothing and offered everything. Some stayed for a season; others are still here today. What mattered was the way each of them helped me remember who I was.

The Wider Circle

My friends and family members showed up in their own ways; they were people who knew when to call, when to listen, and when to simply sit beside me in silence. Their love reminded me that connection doesn't always come from constant contact, but from constant care.

Through them, I learned that being alone isn't the same as being lonely. For the first time, I began to understand that self-love isn't selfish; it's necessary. I used to believe I always needed someone beside me but, over time, I discovered that I was already whole. My friendships gave me the courage to believe in myself again, to stand on my own two feet, and to see failure not as an ending, but as an invitation to begin again.

Reflection

When I look back on those years now, I see that my friendship with Kelly, and so many others, gave me back my sense of self. Divorce stripped away what I thought defined me, but my friends handed me the pieces of confidence and faith I needed until I could stand on my own again. They reminded me that love exists in many forms, and that connection is a sacred act of presence.

Those friendships taught me the essence of connection: showing up, listening, and loving without condition. They became the quiet blueprint for every postcard I would write one day.

Chapter 4

The Transition

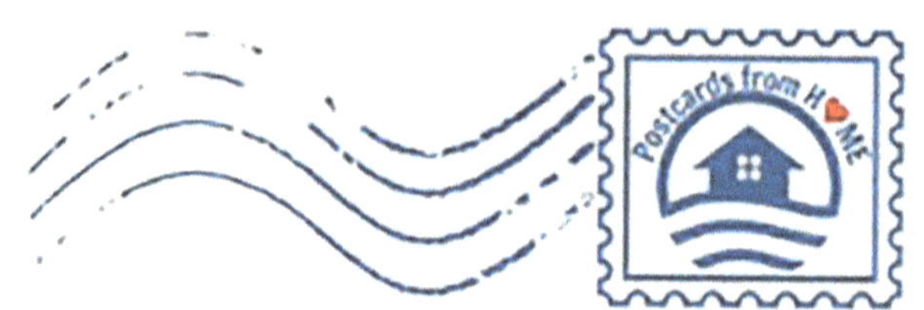

The alarm chimed softly at 4:30 a.m., as it always did. The morning was mine. It had always been. Neither Tanner nor Kallie were ever early risers, so these quiet hours belonged to me. They were my time to wake slowly, sip coffee, take my walk, and let my thoughts settle before the world began to stir.

This morning felt different. The house carried a new kind of silence, not empty, but changed. Tanner was already finding his rhythm in South Bend, surrounded by new faces and new routines. Kallie was still home, asleep in her bedroom just down the hall, soon to begin her junior year. I could hear the faint hum of her fan, steady and soft, a reminder that she was still here, for now.

On the mornings when my children were with their father, the quiet went even deeper. The air seemed heavier, the walls more reflective. My walk on those days felt longer, the stillness pressing in as I tried to find my place in this new rhythm of life. I would pass the same houses and the same trees, yet everything looked slightly different, as though I were learning to see it for the first time. The sound of birds calling from the maple trees, the faint smell of coffee drifting from a neighbor's porch, the dew glistening on lawns, and as fall approached … they all became my anchors. That was the hard part no one prepares you for, holding the ache of missing your children while learning to appreciate the peace that solitude brings.

As I poured my coffee, I reminded myself that transitions are made of small, ordinary moments that can feel both full and lonely. On the table beside me sat a box of postcards, a roll of stamps, a new pen, and my journal. A new beginning waited quietly to take shape.

Learning to Keep Going

Some mornings the silence felt peaceful, and some mornings it ached. During the weeks when Kallie was at her father's, the house seemed to hold its breath. I would walk past her bedroom door, the bed neatly made, and feel a wave of emptiness rise inside me. There were days I sat at the kitchen table with my coffee and cried, not out of weakness, but out of sheer exhaustion.

Holding everything together can feel heavier when no one sees you doing it.

Other days, the quiet almost felt good. I could take a long walk, listen to music, or even say yes to a date. But the dates never lasted. I wanted to believe I was ready, but each time I felt myself pull back. Maybe it was self-protection. Maybe it was loyalty. I had made a promise to my children that I would put them first, and I meant it. That commitment was how I survived. It gave shape to the chaos.

The struggle was real. I worked a full-time job, the kind of position that, in a two-income household, might have padded a retirement account or paid for family vacations, but alone it barely covered rent and bills. The debt from the divorce and the college expenses all seemed endless. Retirement was not a dream I could even imagine then. There were nights when I hated myself for what I thought were my failures as a wife, as a mother, as a woman who could not hold her family together. I never thought about leaving my children or this world; that was never an option. What kept me going were their smiles, the "I love you, Mom," the "thank you for doing that," the small moments that reminded me that even when life felt impossible, love was still present. The little things are often the most important things. I hope you will notice them in your life, too.

People used to tell me that I was like a phoenix rising after every storm. It became a familiar line, one I smiled politely at but never quite believed. I never felt like a phoenix. If I were, I would have flown my children and me straight to a tropical beach somewhere, far from bills, exhaustion, and the weight of doing everything on my own.

The truth is, I did not rise in flames. I rose quietly, one early morning at a time. I went to work, came home, helped with homework, and made dinner. I stretched every dollar, made lists in notebooks, and learned the difference between wants and needs. I smiled through days that were harder than I ever admitted, because that was what I knew how to do, keep moving, keep showing up.

There were seasons when I doubted everything. I questioned my worth, my choices, and wondered whether I had failed the people I loved most. I had been through so many stories by then, heartbreak, betrayal, disappointment, and yet I still tried to find the lesson inside each loss. Maybe that is what people saw when they called me a phoenix. They saw me standing when I could have fallen, laughing when I might have cried, refusing to let pain have the final word.

Even in the hardest seasons, I found ways to celebrate. There were birthdays that always mattered, small dinners that became traditions, and an occasional night out that reminded me life could still hold laughter. Somehow, some way, I made it work. Maybe it was instinct, or maybe it was love. I did what I thought was the right thing, giving my children reasons to smile, and giving myself permission to feel alive again.

Nobody really knew the depth of the self-doubt I carried, how many nights I sat awake doing math in my head, trying to make it all work. Looking back now, I am still not sure how I did it. Little by little, paycheck by paycheck, I paid off the debt. I found steady ground again, not because the storms stopped, but because I learned how to stand in the rain and still believe the sun would come back.

A Mother's Rhythm

When the children were home again, the house filled with life. I cooked real dinners, meals that smelled like home as we sat around the table catching up. I loved those evenings. We talked about classes, friends, and the small triumphs and frustrations of their days. On the mornings after they returned, the house would smell faintly of pancakes or coffee. Shoes by the door, a jacket thrown over a chair, small signs of life and family. And then, just as quickly, the house would grow quiet again when they left. The swing between presence and absence was constant, but over time I stopped resisting it. I learned that love does not fade in the spaces between; it simply changes shape.

I loved being a mother. I still do. It is one of my greatest joys. From the moment I carried my children, through the sleepless nights, to the laughter that still echoes through these rooms, motherhood has been the most challenging and rewarding role of my life.

The pay comes in unexpected ways. A postcard from one of them during a trip that simply says, "Thought of you today, Mom." A surprise call on Tuesday afternoon just to chat. The moments that remind you that all the love you poured out found its way back home. Nothing in this world can match that.

The Writing That Held It All

Over time, the early hours stopped feeling heavy. They became steady. I still woke at 4:30, wrapped my hands around my mug, and let the warmth travel through me while the world outside stirred. Some mornings I prayed. Some mornings I simply sat in silence. I wrote, always.

The postcards had become more than connection; they were a way of breathing. Each one began with a small thought, a piece of home, a snapshot of the day, or a word of encouragement. I did not write to fill space or to impress. I wrote because I loved my children, and because the act of writing reminded me that love still had somewhere to go.

In the beginning, the first few cards to Tanner were simple: updates about the house, Kallie's rehearsals, the weather, what I had made for dinner. Then they began to change. As I settled into the rhythm, the words grew softer, more reflective. Some mornings I shared a quote, others a memory or a story from when they were small. Sometimes all I wrote was, "Thinking of you. Love, M♥M." That was enough.

There was something sacred in putting pen to paper. It slowed me down and taught me to notice the ordinary. I kept postcards everywhere, in the kitchen, in my car, at my desk, ready for whichever space felt right that day. Some mornings I wrote through tears, others through laughter. Writing did not erase loneliness, but it transformed it.

Love is not lessened by distance; it simply travels differently.

What the Transition Taught Me

By the end of Tanner's first month at college, the routine no longer felt new. I stopped counting the days since South Bend. Life had moved forward. There were still moments when the ache returned as I looked at an empty chair, heard a favorite song, or felt the echo of a memory, but those moments no longer hollowed me out. They reminded me that love still lived here.

The postcards began to arrive at Tanner's dorm room regularly. Sometimes Tanner sent a quick photo of one pinned to his wall. Often, he said nothing at all, and that was enough. I did not write for response. I wrote to keep the thread alive. Each card was a whisper across the miles: You are loved. You are remembered. You are never alone.

The writing began to change me. It reminded me that consistency is its own kind of faith, that even when the outcome is uncertain, showing up matters. I began to see that what I thought of as endings were really beginnings in disguise. Family does not disappear when children leave home. It expands. Love does not fade with distance. It stretches and grows.

One morning, as the first light touched the kitchen window, I looked at the small stack of postcards ready to send and realized that the hardest part of letting go had already happened.

The rest was about learning to keep my heart open and to believe that connection could travel farther than I ever imagined.

That is what the transition taught me. Love does not leave. It simply teaches you a new way home.

Chapter 5

Making Waves

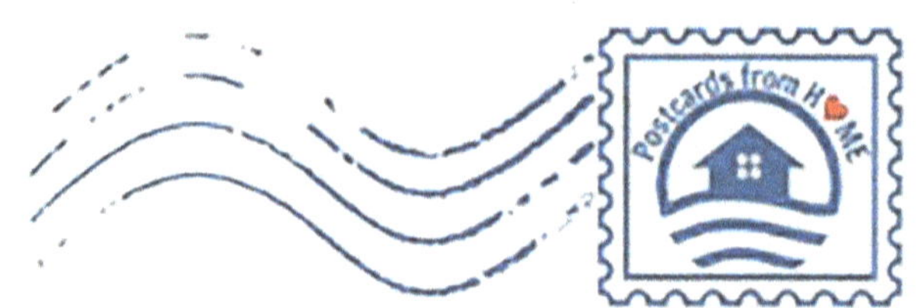

By the time the postcards had become a daily rhythm, I began to sense something larger at play. What started as a simple act of love was becoming a quiet force, one that reached beyond words and distance.

> *"We cannot live only for ourselves. A thousand fibers connect us with our fellow men; and among those fibers, as sympathetic threads, our actions run as causes, and they come back to us as effects."*
>
> \- Herman Melville[1]

What I didn't understand in the early months of writing postcards was that I was creating something far more profound than a communication system. Each morning, as I sat with my coffee and selected a card, I felt as though I was setting in motion invisible waves that reached farther than I could measure.

It began with intention. Not a grand one, but a simple daily choice: to think of my son and, later, my daughter. To wonder how they were doing, what they might need to hear, and what I wanted them to feel. In that quiet moment before pen met paper, something was already moving.

Research is beginning to explore what many of us have long felt to be true: Our thoughts and intentions can influence how we feel and how we relate to others.[2] Research from HeartMath Institute suggests that when we focus on love, care, and appreciation, the rhythm of the heart becomes more coherent, influencing how we feel and relate to those around us.[3] I thought of my children, I was doing more than writing words. I was creating a consistent expression of love and connection.

The Energy of Touch

As my pen moved across the paper, something of me traveled with it. Each letter carried my rhythm and care, a trace of love made visible in ink. The cards became more than messages; they became reminders of how much words mean, not just to me, but to those reading them. When written, love becomes a physical reminder, felt today and held for years to come.

I have always laughed about my handwriting. After seven years of Catholic school at Notre Dame Elementary, my first alma mater, not the same one Tanner attended, I should have had perfect cursive. Instead, my handwriting is part print, part scribble, part emotion. It is uniquely mine, and in its imperfection it is alive. My messy handwriting became my fingerprint of love, instantly recognizable, proof that I was still right there with them.

The physical act of writing added another layer of meaning. Dr. Virginia Berninger's research on handwriting and brain development shows that forming letters by hand activates neural pathways that typing never reaches.[4] When we write by hand, we are not just recording thoughts; we are engaging our bodies in the act of expression.

The Ripple Through Systems

Once written, the postcards entered a network of hands and hearts. The mail carrier who collected them, the postal clerks who sorted them, the delivery staff who placed them in dorm mailboxes, all became part of the journey. Each person, knowingly or not, joined in the passing of love from one human to another.

If everything carries meaning, then those postcards may have changed, even slightly, each time they were touched. The words I wrote carried love into the world, and perhaps some of that love reached people along the way. Whether or not it can be proven, it is beautiful to imagine how a simple message can offer a moment of joy or comfort to someone we may never meet.

Whether or not intention can ever be fully measured, most of us have felt its presence. We know when something is written with care. We sense when words carry thought, time, and attention. The postcards, infused with daily love, moved through the world not just as messages, but as reminders that intention travels with what we create.

The Moment of Reception

The energy found its home when my children opened their mailboxes. Research on mirror neurons suggests that when we observe acts of care, our brains respond in ways that mirror being cared for ourselves.[5] When Tanner or Kallie held one of my postcards, they were not just reading words; they felt the warmth behind them.

The handwriting, the weight of the card, the impressions of the pen, all carried a kind of touch across time and space. Studies on tactile memory show that touch strengthens emotional bonding and security.[6] In that way, each card became a hug they could hold.

The Visible Science of Invisible Connection

Modern research is beginning to explore what many mothers have long understood. Heart rate variability research shows that emotions change the rhythm of the heart, and those patterns can influence others nearby.[7] In physics, there are concepts that describe how particles can remain connected across distance. I don't offer this as proof, but as a metaphor, a way of imagining how connection might persist even when we are far apart.

The postcards became a living example of that connection, what scientists might call quantum entanglement, and what mothers simply call love.

The Web of Witnesses

The ripple didn't end with my children. Every person who came into contact with those cards became part of a larger story. Tanner's dorm rector once told me how much joy it brought him to see those daily deliveries and even asked me to send a few postcards his way, which I happily did. When Kallie went to Nazareth University, the mailroom staff were so touched by the steady stream of cards that one day they slid a piece of purple paper, a pen, and an envelope across the counter to her and said, "This is for you to send a thank you note to your mother for all the postcards she sends you."

She did, and to this day, that note still hangs proudly on the side of my refrigerator, surrounded by other notes and postcards from my children, family, and friends. It is proof that a handwritten message, whether a note, postcard, or letter, will always last longer than any text buried beneath the dozens that follow it.

Her letter reads:

> *"Dear Mom,*
>
> *Thanks for all the postcards ♥. Me and everyone in the mailroom love and appreciate you.*
>
> *You are the best Mom in the world ♥♥.*
>
> *Love, Kallie Ann (chicken)"*

"Chicken" is the nickname we have for each other.

There were also store clerks who began recommending postcards to other families and postal workers who told me how refreshing it was to handle something joyful among the bills and flyers. Each small witness added another ripple to the wave of connection.

Energy Continues

Once I understood this, I became more intentional. Each morning, I focused on the feeling I wanted to send peace, courage, laughter, or love, and trusted that it would reach my children in the way they most needed. Research on the placebo effect shows that belief can influence measurable physiological responses. If belief can influence the body, it can also strengthen connections across distance.

Over time, I came to see that love, when practiced consistently and intentionally, becomes a living energy. It transcends location, logic, and even time. It is what keeps us tethered, and it reminds us that presence can even exist in absence.

The Invisible Made Visible

Science is beginning to explore what many mothers have felt for generations: that love can be felt across distance. It moves through words, thoughts, hands, and hearts. It flows through postal systems and quiet kitchens. It reaches people we may never meet and comforts souls we will never know.

The postcards were my way of living that truth and my way of believing that we are all connected by invisible threads of intention and that small daily acts of love can change the world around us. And each morning, as I continue this practice, I remind myself that I am not just writing cards. I am sending love across time and space, participating in the endless conversation of hearts calling hearts. It is simple, yet powerful.

The energy never stops traveling. The waves never stop expanding. The connection never breaks. I imagine that you, too, have a few stored handwritten notes somewhere in your desk drawer, just waiting for you to read them again, or reply.

And somewhere, in ways that science is only beginning to explain, love always finds its way home.

---

1 Commonly attributed to Herman Melville, most references trace to *Mardi: And a Voyage Thither* (1849). Wording varies by edition; cited here as a period epigraph.

2 B. E. Kok, K. A. Coffey, M. A. Cohn, L. I. Catalino, T. Vacharkulksemsuk, S. B. Algoe, M. Brantley, and B. L. Fredrickson, "How Positive Emotions Build Physical Health: Perceived Positive Social Connections Account for the Upward Spiral Between Positive Emotions and Vagal Tone," Psychological Science 24(7) (2013):1123–1132.

3 D. Childre and H. Martin, The HeartMath Solution (San Francisco: HarperOne, 1999).

4 V. W. Berninger and T. L. Richards, Brain Literacy for Educators and Psychologists (New York: Academic Press, 2002).

[5] M. Iacoboni, Mirroring People: The Science of Empathy and How We Connect with Others (New York: Farrar, Straus & Giroux, 2008).

[6] A. Gallace and C. Spence, "The Science of Interpersonal Touch," *Neuroscience and Biobehavioral Reviews* 34 (2) (2009): 246-259.

[7] R. McCraty, "New Frontiers in Heart Rate Variability and Social Coherence Research," Frontiers in Public Health 5 (2017): article 267.

Chapter 6

The Unexpected Gift of One-on-One Time

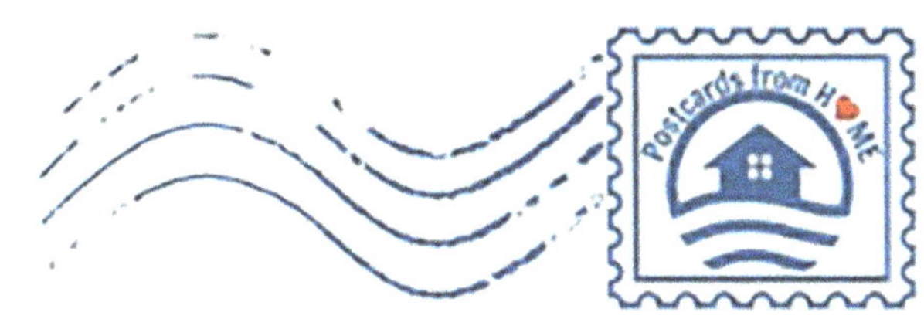

I am blessed with two unique children. Both are smart and funny in their own way, yet each has carved a completely different path. One follows a passion for science and medicine; the other is Broadway bound, drawn to the stage, the lights, and the music. My relationship with each of them is distinct and special, shaped by who they are and what they love.

When Tanner left for college, the house didn't fall silent. The key changed. The rhythm shifted from a trio to a duet performed by Kallie and me. At first it felt strange, too quiet in some ways, too full in others, but slowly we found our harmony. We bumped heads, we laughed until we cried, and we kept learning from each other in ways we never had before.

Having already gone through both heartbreak and the rite of passage that comes with dropping a child off at college, I knew how separation can feel both devastating and sacred. I knew I would be faced with it again in a short two-year time span. I made a conscious decision to make the most of the time I had, with my daughter, with Tanner when he was home, and with my family and friends. It was an awakening of sorts, one that gave me the opportunity to be more present at each moment.

Kallie brings energy and creativity to everything she touches. She doesn't walk into a room; she arrives. She dreams in color and sings in full voice. Her goal of a Broadway career isn't a fantasy; it's a focus. She works hard, balancing rehearsals, classes, and part-time jobs. Before going to college, she would pack her things for her father's house every other week, dragging her feet a little each time. "I just hate switching back and forth," she would sigh, echoing a sentiment no doubt felt by millions of American kids. I understand. Divorce can be hard for young people.

The years after Tanner left for school turned out to be my master class in presence. I noticed the small things, in the way Kallie hummed while studying, how she would flop onto my bed at night sometimes and say, "You're never going to believe this." Sometimes she wanted advice; sometimes she just wanted to be heard. Either way, I listened.

We built a world that was uniquely ours, home cooked meals shared in our cozy kitchen, car rides filled with all sorts of music, and movie nights that often stretched late into the evening. We laughed until our sides hurt, debated over storylines, and forgave each other easily. And when there were tears, they were usually mine. Those moments taught me that love doesn't live in perfection; it lives in showing up, again and again, no matter what. Kallie once said, "Mom, I think that's when we actually became friends." She was right. I've come to understand that the mother-daughter relationship changes as it grows from the nights spent in a rocking chair soothing her, to teaching her how to write or ride a bike, to the countless times I read the opposite role so she could practice her lines. And then, slowly, watching her grow into herself and become the kind of friend I had always dreamed of having in my own child.

Through her, I keep learning the keys I once struggled to play: allowing, acceptance, and patience. Allowing means letting her explore without fixing. Acceptance means seeing her as her own person, not my reflection. Patience means resting in the unknown, trusting that love will carry us through.

Parenting never comes with a handbook. You learn by doing, failing, and trying again. You learn that perfect is a myth and that presence matters more than polish. You learn that self-care isn't selfish; it's a requirement. For single parents, it isn't a luxury.

It's a bill you must pay if you want the lights of love to stay on. You can't pour from an empty cup, and you can't nurture from depletion. I still remind myself of that truth. My children have given me the gift of understanding that balance is just as important as strength.

When Kallie and I visited colleges, the déjà vu is almost comical. On a cold, rainy day, we walk across Nazareth College's campus under one umbrella. She stops, looks around, and says, "This is it. This is where I'm going to get my BFA." I smile through the drizzle. "Then this is where you'll shine," I tell her.

It is another chapter turning, another car to pack, another lesson in letting go. But now I am ready, not because it hurts less, but because I understand what love looks like when it grows up.

"Mom," she asks while shopping for dorm supplies, "I will get postcards too, right?"

"Do you want postcards?"

"Of course I do. But I want to pick out my own!"

We spent the afternoon choosing her favorite Broadway shows, Disney princesses, New York skylines, funny animals. It's her version of connection, her way of owning the tradition. When she leaves for school three-and-a-half hours away, the house grows quiet again, but this time the silence feels sacred. Each morning, I write two postcards: one to Tanner, one to Kallie. Different messages, same heartbeat.

What I Continue to Learn

Life doesn't offer rehearsals; it mirrors what we pour into it. We've all heard the saying, *"When life hands you lemons, make lemonade."*

It still fits, but I've learned that making something sweet out of the bitter takes grit, faith, and choice. That drive can come from your children, from your health, or from that quiet voice inside whispering, *keep going.*

When Tanner first left, I thought I had lost something. What I didn't see then, was how much I would gain. Between the postcards and those two years with Kallie, I discovered the true rhythm of love. Connection isn't built through grand gestures but through consistent presence. Real connection doesn't happen in a single moment. It grows quietly in the spaces where we choose to slow down, notice, and care. It can be found in a shared smile, a kind word, a moment of gratitude, or the stillness of simply listening. These small choices create the same kind of thread that holds families, friendships, and communities together.

Connection is the thread, consistency is the weaving, and love is the fabric that holds it all. When we show up consistently, in both big and small ways, we begin to see that the simplest gestures often carry the deepest meaning. That consistency becomes a habit. People often say it takes twenty-one days to form one. While research shows it can take more or less time depending on the person, the practice, and the purpose, three intentional weeks can still reshape your mindset and set new rhythms in motion.[1] What matters most is not the number of days but the intention you bring to them.

To build a habit of connection, begin by asking yourself:

- Why do I want change?
- Why do I want this in my life?
- Is my *why* strong enough to carry me through when the first spark fades?

Twenty-one days of deliberate, heart-centered action can plant the roots of something lasting. It may take less time for some and longer for others, but transformation always begins with intention. Connection works the same way. Whether it's with your child, your partner, your faith, or yourself, it's the small, repeated acts that reshape your world. The habit of love, practiced daily, becomes the rhythm of a life that feels whole.

Love evolves. Families grow, change, adapt, and learn to accept.

Connection is a daily act of:

- showing up
- allowing
- accepting
- practicing patience
- extending forgiveness

These remain my compass points.

Letting go is its own kind of love. Allowing, accepting, and forgiving yourself and others are the quiet acts that hold everything together.

I'm not a perfect mother. No one is.

But I chose to:

- show up consistently
- make it tangible
- give without expectation

I work hard.
I love harder.

And if you're reading this, whether you're a parent feeling distant from your child or a child feeling far from home, please know it's never too late. Maybe you don't know what to say. Maybe too much time has passed. That's okay.

Start small. Send a postcard. Write a note.

Do it once a day, maybe even for twenty-one days.

You may not get a response right away, but something will shift. Maybe the phone will ring. Maybe a card or postcard from the other person will appear in your mailbox.

Kallie said while I was writing this book, "People underestimate what a handwritten message can do. It's not about what's written, it's that someone took the time. If you're reading this book and thinking of your mom, send her a note. She'll keep it forever."

She's right. Love keeps showing up, quietly, persistently, until the world softens enough to receive it.

If you need help finding the words, visit my website and explore *The Journey Back Home*, a set of postcards and messages created for anyone ready to rebuild a bridge, start a conversation, or simply remind someone that love still lives at the same address.

Love doesn't vanish with silence. It waits.

And sometimes, all it takes is a stamp and a little courage to find its way home.

What This Became

Sometimes the most powerful things in life are so simple, we overlook them.

Over time, I felt compelled to share this with everyone reading this book, in the hope that even one family might feel more connected, one relationship might be restored, one person might feel a little less alone, and perhaps more than that.

It is something that can be done by anyone: mothers, fathers, family members, and friends.

Anyone who wants to stay connected with the people they love. Anyone who may have fallen out of touch and doesn't know how to begin again.

I didn't set out to create a system.

I wasn't trying to build anything. But over time, through years of showing up one postcard at a time, something took shape. A way of staying connected that was simple, consistent, and intentional. A way to reach across distance without pressure.

A way to show up without interrupting someone's independence. A way to remind someone they matter without needing anything in return. This is what I have come to call the **Postcard Method**.

It is not complicated. It is not time-consuming. But it is powerful.

It is built on three simple ideas:

Show up consistently

Connection is not built through occasional effort. It is built through small, repeated acts over time.

Make it tangible

A handwritten message creates something real. Something that can be held, saved, and returned to.

Give without expectation

There is no pressure to respond. No obligation. Just a steady presence that says, I am here.

During my children's college years, I sent approximately 1,200 postcards. I never counted as I went. I just kept writing.

Because it was never about the number. It was about consistency. More than 900 of them were saved. Not because they were perfect, but because they meant something to them.

Because they showed up. Because they were real.

Looking back now, I understand this:

Connection across distance is not built through big moments. It is maintained through small, consistent acts that remind someone you are still there.

---

[1] P. Lally, C. H. M. van Jaarsveld, H. W. W. Potts, and J. Wardle, "How Are Habits Formed: Modelling Habit Formation in the Real World," European Journal of Social Psychology 40(6) (2010):998–1009.

Chapter 7

The Power of the Written Word

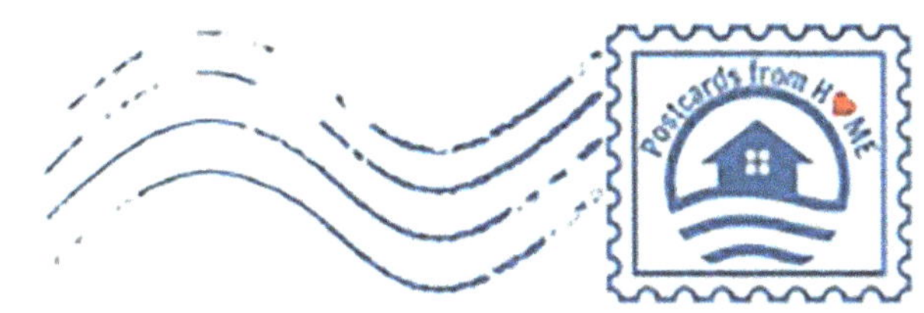

Think of a time when you were going home after a long day. There was the drive back from work, the errands, the endless list of to-dos that never quite feels done. You pull into the driveway, instinctively step out of the car, and walk to the mailbox, already anticipating the pile of recyclables you'll have. The usual suspects: advertisements for new siding and new roofs, another credit card offer, a grocery flyer promising a sale that never seems to end.

Then, just as you flip through the stack, you stop.

Nestled between the noise is something different: a small 4" × 6" postcard, a soft, beautiful photograph of the ocean with "*Wish You Were Here",* written across the sand in coral script. You hold it like a tiny treasure, its edges warm from your fingers. You can't help yourself, you flip it over immediately, eager to see who thought of you, what they said, where they were when they wrote it.

"Oh, my goodness," you breathe. "They thought of me."

You carry it inside like a prized possession. Maybe you show it to whoever's home, or if no one's there, you call your friend the sender to thank them, to tell them how much it meant. Maybe you pin it to the refrigerator, so you'll see it each morning, a reminder that you are loved, that you have people who care.

And I know you've got one somewhere, a postcard tucked in a drawer, slipped between the pages of a book, saved because it mattered.

Not long ago, I was wandering through an old bookstore, Lyrical Ballads in Saratoga Springs, New York, the kind of place that smells like paper, dust, and stories. As I thumbed through boxes of vintage postcards, I asked the owner why he carried them.

He smiled and said, "They're antiques. Nobody writes postcards anymore." I smiled right back and said, "You just wait and see. That's about to change."

I bought a few postcards that day. One was a photograph of Notre Dame Church, the same church that stood in the town where I grew up. No irony there, I thought. For the three dollars it cost, I brought that postcard home to my parents, and we talked about how, even though none of us were alive in the 1930s, that old church looked almost exactly the same.

As we talked, I found myself tracing the faded handwriting on another card, words written by someone long gone, yet still alive in ink. We wondered if we might have known their family, or if our paths had ever crossed. The conversation that flowed from those few lines reminded me once again of the quiet power that lives in the written word.

My eyes began to well up as I wrote this, realizing how powerful, how sacred, that connection truly is. A postcard that someone else had written decades ago stirred something still living in me. How would you feel knowing that, maybe years from now, someone might pick up a postcard you wrote because they were inspired just enough to hold on to it?

That's legacy. That's the ripple.

When was the last time you felt that kind of anticipation about a text message?

Have you ever?

There is power in the written word, and you just proved it to yourself.

So, ask yourself now: Who do I want to connect with, reconnect with, or simply bring a smile to?

The Difference You Can Hold

We live in a world of instant everything. I can text my children and get a response before I've put my phone down, or watch that dreaded "read" notification appear with no reply, creating the kind of anxiety that handwritten words never generate. We send emails that arrive faster than we can walk to the kitchen, often typed with predictive text that finishes our thoughts before we do. We share our lives in real time through posts and stories that vanish after twenty-four hours.

But there's something different about a handwritten word that all our technology, for all its magic, can't replicate. When you hold a handwritten postcard, you're holding something real. You can feel the slight pressure where the pen pressed into paper.

There's weight to it, not just physical, but emotional weight. It smells like ink, sometimes faintly of the sender's home. It takes up space in your hands in ways no digital message ever will.

We're living in an age of connection paradox. We're more linked than ever through technology, yet loneliness is at epidemic levels. We can reach anyone instantly, yet we struggle to truly reach anyone at all.

Walk into any restaurant and count the families staring at screens instead of each other, while the toddler is propped up watching videos, learning young that stimulation comes from a screen. Notice how many people check their phones while walking, missing the world around them. We may have more ways of being connected now, but I would ask: Connected to what? Is it meaningful connection? Perhaps it's connection to our phones, to the comparison trap we fall into on social media, or to the constant barrage of reels for items we don't need. We're more connected and more disconnected than ever.

That's why the written word matters more now, not less. In a sea of digital noise, a handwritten message is a life raft. In a world of instant and disposable, something crafted and lasting stands out. In a culture where everyone is talking through screens, the quiet arrival of a postcard feels like someone is actually listening.

When we receive something handwritten, we stop. We put down our phones. Research shows that physical mail captures our attention differently than digital messages. we spend more time with it, engage with it more deeply, and remember it longer.[1]

Studies have found that receiving handwritten notes can boost mood and even increase serotonin levels, the brain chemical associated with happiness and well-being.[2]

For those few moments, the scroll stops. The comparison trap pauses. We're present with something real, something someone took time to create just for us. That moment of presence, even if brief, reminds us what genuine connection feels like. The tactile experience of holding paper, seeing handwriting, reading words meant only for you creates what researchers call a "pattern interrupt," a break in our automatic digital habits that allows us to be fully present.[3]

This is your invitation to break out that postcard you've been holding onto for some time and send it.

Write a postcard. Change a life.

Why Writing by Hand Matters More Than Ever

According to the American College Health Association's Spring 2023 National College Health Assessment, 35 percent of college students reported having been diagnosed with anxiety, and 27 percent reported having been diagnosed with depression.[4] Many students struggle with mental health issues, feeling alone despite being surrounded by thousands of peers and more digital connections than any generation in history.

In this landscape of digital overwhelm and genuine loneliness, a handwritten postcard becomes more than just mail. It becomes proof that someone sees you, that you matter enough for someone to find paper and pen, to sit down and form letters with their hand, to walk to a mailbox.

When you write by hand, everything slows down. Your thoughts can't race ahead of your fingers the way they do when typing. There's no autocorrect changing your words, no delete key tempting you to perfect every sentence. You have to commit, to each word, each letter, and each message.

Research shows that physically writing things down enhances memory retention, engaging different parts of the brain and creating deeper connections to the content.[5] Beyond the science, there's the soul of it. Your handwriting is uniquely yours.

My children know my lowercase a's, the way my y's loop, how my writing changes when I'm tired or excited. They're reading me, not just my words.

The Journey of Love Through Mail

Every postcard takes a journey that digital messages never will. It starts with intentionally selecting the right card, finding a pen, clearing a space to write. Already, before a single word is written, you've invested more effort than a hundred texts require.

Then comes the writing itself. Your hand moves across paper, leaving traces of yourself in ink, the indentations where you pressed harder, the curve of your letters, the occasional smudge that proves a human, not a machine, created this.

After you write it, address it, and stamp it, you walk to the mailbox. You're physically carrying your love to a launching point, where it will be picked up, sorted, and travel through hands and machines, across miles and time zones, until it lands in another mailbox. And there, the magic completes itself. Someone walks to get their mail, reaches in, pulls out this tangible piece of love, then holds what you once held. Their fingers touch where yours touched as well. The circle closes.

What I Learned from Writing So Many Postcards

After years of daily postcards, I've discovered truths that surprised me. Writing to my children didn't just maintain our connection. It transformed it. And it transformed me. First, I became more observant. When you commit to writing daily, you start collecting moments worth sharing, the funny thing your coworker said, the way the light hit the trees on your morning drive, the small victories and tiny absurdities that normally pass unmentioned. I kept a notebook beside me and added little reminders about upcoming tests, shows, or events, tiny threads I could weave into my messages later.

Second, I learned that consistency creates its own form of love. Some days I wrote profound things, other days, the simplest notes. My children once told me there was never a boring postcard; it was always a joy to get mail.

Third, the constraint of postcard space taught me the economy of love. No room for lectures or overwhelming emotion, just enough space for what matters most:

Thinking of you. Proud of you. The dog misses you (I do too).

Less can be more.

Your Invitation to Write

If at some point you received a handwritten postcard, letter, or note, did you keep it? Did you put it in a special box or on the fridge? Did you call and thank the person who sent it? If you said yes to one of those things, maybe it's time to start writing again, not a text or an email, but a handwritten message.

Think of someone who might need a smile today and send something to them.

Maybe it's your child away at college. Maybe it's a parent in a nursing home. Maybe it's a friend going through hard times, someone in the military, a neighbor who seems lonely. Or maybe it's you yourself. You can write postcards to yourself, creating a record of your days, your growth, your journey.

People often ask if it ever felt expensive, after all, stamps and postcards can add up over time. The truth is, it doesn't have to feel that way. There are simple, affordable ways to send something through the mail, and even the smallest cost can carry great meaning. When I think of it like that, it feels less like an expense and more like an investment, in love, in connection, in presence.

I never once said, "This is expensive; I'm not doing this anymore." I could have, but I didn't. I simply looked for what fit my budget at the time. I still remember the day I bought a roll of one hundred postcard stamps. The clerk looked at me as if to say, *Why on earth would you need that many?* I smiled and said, "I send a postcard to my children every day." Then came the pause, the puzzled expression, and I just chuckled and said, "Have a great day."

What I wanted was a simple communication channel to my children that would last. Not just when they receive the postcard, but when they read it again later, a week, a month, or even a year down the road. That one small investment, a postcard and a stamp that might be read two or three times, shared, and touched by others, ended up costing just pennies a day.

I'm not here to sell anything. I'm here to connect. People have choices. You can go right to the post office, grab a handful of postcards, and begin sending them out. Those pre-stamped postcards might not have flowery sentiment or the beautiful scene, but I've used them, and whether in a pinch or simply by choice, they work. Our words, our love, and our message still travel. So, no matter which postcard you choose, it all begins with your intention.

And if you're drawn to more meaningful designs cards created to carry love, reflection, and everyday presence, you can explore the ones I've created on my website. Each design grew from this same practice, born from handwritten moments that built bridges between hearts. Whether you choose mine, the post offices, or one you make yourself, what matters most is that you begin.

Connection doesn't start with the card. It starts with the heart holding the pen.

And while we all make choices about how we spend our time and money, it is easy for priorities to drift without us even noticing. Small habits add up, often pulling our attention away from what matters most. For me, this simple daily ritual was never about cost. It was about connections.

The Legacy of Letters

Years from now, texts will be lost in old phones. Emails will be buried in digital archives. Social media posts will vanish into the void of deleted accounts and platform changes. But those postcards? They'll be in boxes, in drawers, in frames. They'll be pulled out and read again. They'll be evidence that in a fast world, someone took the slow way to say *you matter.*

My children have kept nearly every postcard, more than a thousand pieces of mail tracing their college years, their growth, and our parallel journeys. They are more than a record of days; they are proof of presence, proof that every single day, no matter what else happened that day, they were worth the time I took to write.

One Christmas, my son made a collage featuring his first and last Notre Dame postcards, surrounded by selected others. When I opened it, I cried, of course. The power of those written words became a gift once again, this time for me to cherish. It now hangs proudly in my bedroom, where I often look, pause, and smile.

The written word holds power, not in brute strength, but in its timeless ability to carry courage, hope, encouragement, love, compassion, friendship, determination, joy, and countless other gifts. Its power travels across miles and moments, touching hearts along the way.

There were times, as I wrote each postcard, when I thought, *I hope these words can give them the hug I cannot give today*. That is the quiet magic of the written word, it moves through us and between us. You hold that same power, both for yourself and for others.

Who will you write to?

---

1 Canada Post, *A Bias for Action: The Neuroscience Behind the Response-Driving Power of Direct Mail* (Canada Post Corporation, 2015).

2 A. Kumar and N. Epley, "Undervaluing Gratitude: Expressers Misunderstand the Consequences of Showing Appreciation," Psychological Science 29(9) (2018):1423–1435.

3 C. Duhigg, The Power of Habit: Why We Do What We Do in Life and Business (New York: Random House, 2012), 62–67.

4 American College Health Association, American College Health Association-National College Health Assessment III: Reference Group Executive Summary (Spring 2023), accessed November 21, 2025.

5 A. L. H. van der Meer and F. R. van der Weel, "Handwriting but not Typewriting Leads to Widespread Brain Connectivity: A High-Density EEG Study," Frontiers in Psychology 14 (2024):1219945.

Chapter 8

Finding Your Happy

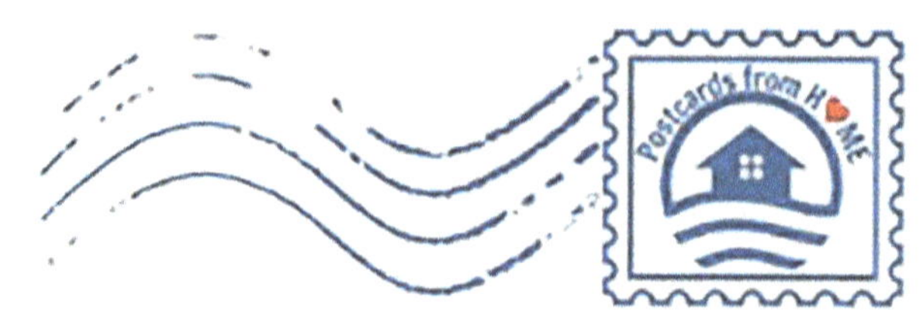

Once the pomp and circumstance of graduations were over and my children were settled into their new chapters, I stood in my kitchen one quiet morning and thought, "*Where do I go from here?*"

I had friends, a job, a dog, and a career, all good things. Yet something inside me felt unsteady, as though the rhythm of my life had changed overnight. For more than twenty years, I had dedicated myself to being a mother. I loved nearly every moment of it, but this was different.

After one graduation ceremony, my former husband gave me a hug and said, "You did a good job, Sandy." Those words caught me off guard. I nearly cried. They were simple, but they mattered. I did not need validation, yet hearing those words filled me with deep gratitude. Kindness, even after endings, can still heal. It reminded me of the good moments, of what we had done right, and of how love changes form but never disappears.

That morning in my kitchen, I thought about all the years of parenting, the late-night calls, the football games, the performances, the postcards, the countless drives and visits. The joy, the chaos, the tears, and the laughter that made up our family story. I realized that this next chapter was mine to write. My role as a mother would never end; it would simply evolve. My children were stepping into their futures, and I was being called to step fully into my own.

I knew who I was. I was choosing to step into who I was becoming.

The Deeper Break

For much of my marriage, I believed that fairytales could come true. And although the man I married was not my prince charming, I still believed. People come together for many reasons, and I have come to realize that in our case one of the reasons was to show me how resilient I could be and to bring into this world the two most extraordinary human beings I know, my children.

Divorce reveals more than endings. It reveals truth. It uncovers who people are when life no longer fits the picture they imagined. It shows what they valued, what they feared, and sometimes what they never truly saw in each other. In the wake of my divorce, I went through every emotion imaginable: anger, disbelief, sadness, loneliness, rejection, and a kind of hollow grief that words can barely describe. What many do not acknowledge is the anguish divorce creates in the one who trusts. It breaks something deep inside. It makes you question your worth, your judgment, and your ability to love again.

The relationships that followed were not failures. They were reflections of my unfinished healing. I was still carrying pieces of the past I had not yet forgiven. I was still clinging to the only identity I knew how to embody without hesitation: being a mother. And by faith and determination, I was going to do that part right.

My children never asked for any of it. They simply landed in the storm. I rose again, as I always had, and mothered through the ache. There were nights I cried quietly in the kitchen, mornings when I called my friend Kelly or my family just to find a steady voice on the other end of the line. But no matter how heavy it became, I found a way to keep going.

Looking back now, I see that every choice, even the painful ones, shaped who I have become. My children are grown, carving their own lives, and I am learning to embrace myself, not only as a mother, but as a woman who has walked through heartbreak, found forgiveness, and chosen to keep love alive.

I can stand in the mirror now, smile through the lines that time has written, and know that I have already survived my hardest days.

Learning to Be Present

For years, I had been busy raising children, rebuilding after my divorce, proving I could handle it all. And when the busyness of active motherhood finally lifted, I did what I had always done: I filled the space with more noise.

I scrolled through strangers' lives on my phone. I kept my calendar packed. I listened to podcasts while I cooked and checked email while I walked. I told myself I was staying connected, but the truth was simpler and sadder: I had forgotten how to be still.

There is a difference between being busy and being present. Between filling time and inhabiting it. I had been so afraid of what I might feel in the silence that I never gave myself the chance to find out.

But slowly, something shifted. I started leaving my phone in another room. I walked without headphones. I smiled at strangers and noticed when they smiled back.

These small acts felt revolutionary because they required something I had lost, and that was my attention.

Real connection, I realized, does not come from staying busy or staying plugged in. It comes from showing up for yourself, for the moment, for the person in front of you. When you walk down the street with your eyes down, scrolling, you miss the opportunity to see and be seen. You miss the chance to connect.

Research by Dr. Sherry Turkle shows that our constant connectivity has actually made us less connected, less able to be present with ourselves and others[1]. The empty nest had forced me to confront what I had been avoiding: not loneliness, but stillness. Not isolation, but presence.

And in that stillness, I finally began to hear my own voice.

Looking Inward

For years, I had been searching. I read everything I could find, books on healing, spirituality, growth, happiness. I filled notebooks with insights and ideas. I was always learning, always reaching for the next answer, the next framework that might finally help me understand how to be whole.

But I was looking in the wrong direction.

There is wisdom in books, of course. There are teachers and mentors who light the way. But somewhere in all that seeking, I had forgotten the most fundamental truth: Happiness does not come from outside. It lives within us, waiting to be recognized.

There are millions of people on this earth, and we are all uniquely ourselves. No book could tell me who Sandra was. No expert could hand me my own dreams. The answers I was searching for were not hidden in someone else's words. They were buried beneath years of my own noise, my own doing, my own devotion to everyone but myself. It was not until I stopped filling every moment, with busyness, with other people's wisdom, with the relentless pursuit of external answers, that I could finally hear my own voice.

One of the most transformative moments during this time came in an executive-coaching session. I was asked a question I had never truly considered:

Who is Sandra, not mom, not ex-wife, not employee, but Sandra?

The silence that followed was deafening. I realized I had spent decades defining myself through the roles I filled, not the person I was. That question opened something in me. It wasn't about career goals or leadership, it was an invitation to meet myself again. To listen. To name what mattered. That session was the beginning of a new kind of work, the inner work. It didn't happen all at once. But over time, it helped me uncover the courage to ask different questions, the kind that can't be answered on a résumé:

What do I love? What do I need? What do I believe in?

Self-Discovery

As I grew quieter inside, I began to truly see myself. For years my care naturally centered on my children. Now, for the first time, I could turn that same devotion inward.

I explored new interests, revisited old passions, and let curiosity lead me. I read books on human behavior, spirituality, and the science of energy. I discovered how thought and emotion shape what we attract into our lives. The idea that intention and attention can shift what is possible fascinated me. Modern science was finally explaining what spiritual traditions had taught for centuries, that everything is connected.[2]

Through this process, I learned something profound. The hurts, fears, and memories I carried lived only in my own mind. They were mine to release. Holding on to them only weighed me down, serving no purpose other than to keep me from joy.

I had to pause when I realized that truth. I do not have to carry what no longer belongs to me. I am worthy of happiness. You are worthy of happiness. Fill your mind with good connections, with joyful thoughts, with the best parts of your day. This is your story. You hold the pen.

Writing It All Down

When I began to journal again, I rediscovered something I had long forgotten: Writing clears the mind and softens the heart. There is something sacred about putting words on paper without judgment, without worrying about perfection. It is where truth begins to take shape. I did not write to be profound. I wrote to be free. Some pages were messy, some full of gratitude, some written through tears. But in that practice, I found a rhythm of healing that no conversation or advice could ever match. Writing became my quiet form of prayer, a space where I could meet myself honestly.

Research by Dr. James Pennebaker shows that expressive writing, even just a few minutes a day, can strengthen emotional regulation, improve physical health, and help people make sense of their lives.[3] I did not know that at the time, but I felt it.

Through journaling, I began to see patterns in my thoughts, dreams, and fears. I noticed that what I focused on grew stronger. Gratitude deepened, clarity returned, and peace slowly replaced restlessness.

Writing connected me not only to my own heart but to every person who has ever put pen to paper in search of understanding.

Finding My Purpose

Throughout my life I have read countless books on self-care, healing, and mindfulness. Each one offered something small, but together they taught me that happiness isn't a single discovery. It's a practice.

During my journaling, I began creating a list one hundred things that made me happy. It started simply:

- Smelling lilacs in the spring
- Dancing in the kitchen
- Watching the stars
- The sound of the ocean
- Fresh coffee in the morning
- Laughing with friends
- Cooking from scratch
- Long walks and good conversation
- Music that moves me
- The feeling of clean sheets

At first, the list came easily. The first ten or twenty things appeared almost instantly. But then it began to go deeper, like peeling back the layers of an onion or taking down a brick wall, brick by brick, to uncover what had been blocking my happiness. Each new layer revealed something smaller, simpler, more personal.

Once I had filled the page, I set it aside for a few days. Then I returned to it and began sorting my list into categories, nature, music, creativity, connection, faith, curiosity. I wanted to see where the patterns led me. Some people find that their list leans toward adventure or learning, others toward stillness or beauty. There is no wrong answer. The idea is not perfection; it's awareness.

After that, I began to play with the lists. If these were the things that brought me joy, how could I bring more of them into my daily life? For some, that might mean planting a garden or taking a painting class. For others, it might mean volunteering, learning something new, or simply spending more time outside.

This practice can become a powerful tool for reflection or even for change. I've used it in my coaching work with people trying to rediscover purpose or direction.

Some go further and ask, *what could I do for a living that would make me happy?* and then write down specific paths that align with their lists. It becomes not only a reminder of joy, but a map for possibility.

And it doesn't have to be one hundred. It can be fifty, or twenty, or whatever number feels right. There is no wrong way to do this. What matters is the noticing the act of honoring what makes your heart lift. When you are at peace with who you are, from the inside out, and when you hold gratitude for the little things, happiness follows. Happiness looks different for everyone. It may not resonate with you in the same way it does for someone else, and that's perfectly fine. It's not meant to. What matters is that it's yours. This practice, shared by many teachers of mindfulness and self-awareness, has been shown to cultivate gratitude, strengthen confidence, and reinforce emotional resilience.[4]

Happiness, I realized, isn't something to chase. It's something to remember.

[1] S. Turkle, *Reclaiming Conversation: The Power of Talk in a Digital Age* (New York: Penguin Press, 2015). pp. 1-7

[2] "Science of the Heart: Exploring the Role of the Heart in Human Performance," HeartMath Research Center, HeartMath Institute, accessed November 21, 2025, https://www.heartmath.org/research/science-of-the-heart/.

[3] J. W. Pennebaker, *Opening Up: The Healing Power of Expressing Emotions* (New York: Guilford Press, 1997) pp. 3-7

[4] R. A. Emmons and M. E. McCullough, "Counting Blessings Versus Burdens: An Experimental Investigation of Gratitude and Subjective Well-Being." *Journal of Personality and Social Psychology* 84(2) (2003): 377–389.

Chapter 9

The Recognition

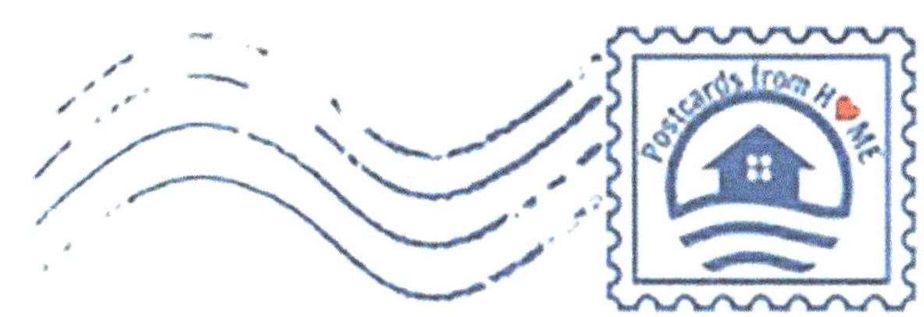

For a long while after my kids left home, I still couldn't see my authentic self. I was so busy trying to figure out my next chapter that I didn't realize I was already writing it.

The postcards I had been writing for years were more than a way to stay connected with my children. They were an authentic expression of who I am at my core. Being a mother is authentic, yes, but I am more than that role. I am love. I am the energy that flows from my mind through the pen and onto the paper, and now into this book. I am someone who cares deeply, who shows up consistently, who finds creative ways to encourage and support the people I love. I am someone who believes in the power of small, daily acts of love. I am energy seeking to do good, to create connections, and to spread hope across any distance.

The Evolution of Relationships

One of the most unexpected gifts of learning to be alone was how it transformed my relationships with others. When you are comfortable with solitude, you stop relating out of fear or neediness and start choosing connection because you genuinely want it, not because you require it for emotional survival. You love more purely, listen more deeply, and serve more freely. Authenticity gives others permission to be real.

Time alone also changes the questions you ask. Not "How can I fill this emptiness?" but "What is this emptiness teaching me?" Not "Who will I be without my children at home?" but "Who have I always been underneath all the caregiving?" The answers do not appear overnight; they emerge in stillness and patience.

In my time of solitude, my relationships with my children deepened in ways I had not anticipated. Because I was no longer clinging to them as my primary source of identity and purpose, I could relate to them more as individuals and less as extensions of myself. My friendships changed, too. I became more selective about how I spent my social energy, more willing to have honest conversations, and more able to show up authentically rather than performing the version of myself I thought others wanted to see. Research by Dr. Brené Brown on vulnerability and authentic connection shows that our capacity for genuine intimacy is directly related to our comfort with ourselves.[1] And research by Dr. Reed Larson on solitude and psychological development shows that people who are comfortable being alone display higher creativity, stronger emotional regulation, and greater resilience.[2] Learning to be alone is not about filling space. It is preparation for living with purpose.

The Joy of Solitude

Perhaps the most surprising discovery for me during this time was that solitude could be joyful, not just tolerable. There is joy in choosing for yourself what to eat, when to rest, what to pursue. There is joy in the silence itself, in hearing your own thoughts, in noticing the sounds outside your window that were always there but hidden beneath the family noise.

There is joy in rediscovering that you are interesting company for yourself. Your own thoughts, humor, and observations can keep you engaged for hours. You do not need constant validation to feel content and alive.

Finding your way to the joy of living authentically means shedding the layers that never belonged to you. It means letting go of the voices that said you were not enough, or that shining too brightly might make others uncomfortable. When those thoughts return, stop, quiet your mind, be still, and listen to your heart. Remember how much you love yourself. You are here, and there is a reason for that.

When you live authentically, people notice. Energy feels different. The rector at Notre Dame who missed seeing the postcards each day and the mailroom staff at my daughter's college who encouraged her to write me a thank-you note. These were small but meaningful signs that authenticity does touch others. When you show up as yourself, without apology, you invite others to do the same.

Another benefit of living authentically is that it changes our understanding of abundance as we recognize that true wealth does not come from money or partnership. It comes from meaning, connection, and presence. Wholeness does not require another person to complete us. When we live authentically, we need less. We measure abundance in connection, gratitude, and peace rather than possessions or approval.

Meditation taught me to notice when I slipped into comparison or self-criticism and to gently redirect my attention to what is true: "I am," I found myself repeating.

If you are caught in comparison culture, take a breath and remember this: True comparison is impossible. No one else has lived your life, and you have not lived theirs. Social media amplifies the illusion of perfection, showing curated joy while concealing private struggle. Everyone is fighting unseen battles and celebrating victories you cannot see. Your journey, your timeline, and your gifts are uniquely yours.

What Finding Your Happy Actually Looks Like

My life did not drastically change after I found my authentic self. I still work, write, and walk with my golden retriever, Knute, who has mastered the art of being unselfconsciously happy in every moment. But everything feels different because I am different.

I now trust in a higher power call it God, the Universe, or whatever name fits your spirit, and I trust that there is a plan. Finding your happiness does not mean your problems vanish; it means you stop fighting against who you are and begin working with your true nature. When I stopped trying to be who I thought others wanted me to be and began honoring who I truly am, everything shifted. Confidence came. Clarity came. Purpose followed.

I took a lesson from the birds: Birds do not worry about their next meal, nor do they compare nests. They trust the process, and they fly. Nature shows us time and again that there are seasons for everything: growth and rest, abundance and quiet preparation. The empty-nest season is not a loss; it is an invitation. Fighting against it, filling every moment to avoid silence, only robs us of its gifts. The next time you see a bird with a worm, take it as your reminder to trust. Trust that your authentic self is enough. Trust that your gifts matter. Trust that the world needs exactly what you have to offer, given in the way only you can give it.

Preparation for Purpose

I now realize that those months of solitude were not a waste of time. They were necessary preparation for something greater, and they were a bridge from who I was to who I am becoming. From defining myself through roles to discovering myself through truth.

Everything I endured, the good, the hard, and the broken, brought me here. The postcards began as a way to maintain connection with my children but evolved into a discipline of authentic expression, proof that small, consistent acts of love can ripple outward in ways we may never see. Solitude made room for purpose to emerge.

The Ongoing Journey

If even one person reads this and feels less alone, then I have done what I came here to do. The postcards were never just about my children. They were about being who I am: someone who is love, someone who believes in the power of connection across any distance. I came to understand that learning to be alone is not a destination but an ongoing practice. Even now, I keep discovering new layers of myself and new ways that solitude serves me and those around me.

If you find yourself standing in a quiet home, coffee in hand, asking "Now what?"

Know that you are not at the end. You are at the beginning. Write out your one hundred things. Shed the layers that no longer serve you. Trust like the birds. The silence is not empty. It is full of everything you have been too busy to hear.

---

1 Brené Brown, Daring Greatly: How the Courage to Be Vulnerable Transforms the Way We Live, Love, Parent, and Lead (New York: Gotham Books, 2012).

2 Reed Larson, "The Solitary Side of Adolescence," New Directions for Child and Adolescent Development (1997); see also Reed Larson, "Social Isolation and the Development of Autonomy," Journal of Youth and Adolescence (1990).

Chapter 10

The Invitations

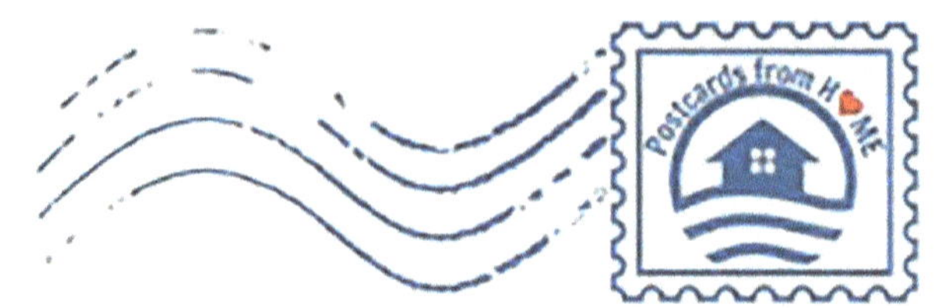

With each page you have turned and each chapter you have read, I wonder if you found yourself thinking, *I have struggled too.* Maybe you recognized yourself in moments of transition, in trying to figure out who you are again, or at least trying to. Maybe you paused, thinking of your son or daughter, remembering what that moment felt like or imagining the day that is still ahead.

If any of those felt familiar, I want you to hear this clearly: you are not alone. I have been there. And so have more people than we ever say out loud.

Life has a way of closing chapters, whether we are ready or not. Divorce. Change. Letting go of identities we once worked hard to hold together. These moments can leave us feeling proud and exhausted at the same time, hopeful and emptied out. But life does not stop when a chapter closes. It begins again, quietly, in the space that follows, when we are left to decide how we will keep going.

When my children were young, I used to remind them that each day is a present. Yesterday is already behind us. Tomorrow is not yet here. All we truly have is today. A single day wrapped and waiting to be opened. Even in seasons when I felt unsure or worn down, that belief grounded me. It reminded me that I still had a choice in how I showed up. That I could open the day with intention and make the present, imperfect as it might be, the best day I could.

That belief is what brings us here.

What follows are a few simple invitations. You are free to accept any of them, all of them, or none of them.

The First Invitation: Inward

Pause for a moment.
Stop.
Breathe.

Think about the person or people who kept crossing your mind as you read these pages. Listen to what your heart has been trying to say. Not what you think you *should* say, but what feels true. What has been waiting quietly for your attention.

The Second Invitation: Outward

Many of us carry words we never say. We tell ourselves we will reach out later, when there is more time, more energy, or when the right words come. But later often becomes silence, and silence can make even the strongest among us feel invisible.

You do not need perfect words or special supplies. A postcard is lovely, but it is not required. Tear a page from an old notebook. Use the envelopes tucked away in a drawer, the ones you have kept without knowing why. You already have everything you need.

Write honestly. Write imperfectly. Write with intention. Then mail it. Send your words to someone who matters to you, someone you love, someone you miss, or someone who needs to know they are not alone. Let your words travel.

The Third Invitation: Shared

If you choose to send a postcard to me, it will be included on a world map on my website, showing how words move through the world and how many people, in different places and different seasons of life, were moved to reconnect and write from the heart. A postcard is simply those words, a moment, and a place.

Your name does not need to be included unless you wish it to be. If you prefer your postcard to appear without identifying details, you may indicate that on the card itself. The choice is always yours.

That map exists as a quiet reminder. A way of seeing that others have been here too. That connection is not rare. That a small, handwritten act still matters.

Sometimes seeing that others have paused, written, and reached out is enough to remind us that we are not alone. That life continues, even after difficult chapters. That showing up, in the simplest ways, can matter.

There is no obligation. Only an open door.

Sandra Tarkleson
Postcards from H♥ME
PO Box 93
Malone, NY 12953

What matters most is not where the postcard goes, but that it is written. That you stopped long enough to listen. That you chose presence and care in a world that often rushes past both.

Sometimes a few handwritten words are enough to interrupt the silence, soften what someone is carrying, and remind us that love still travels, that distance does not diminish meaning, and that even the smallest acts can ripple farther than we ever imagine. How to send your postcard

HOW TO SEND YOUR POSTCARD

If you wish to send me a postcard, please use format below:

Write anything you'd like to share, a reflection, a message, or what this book meant to you.

Postcards sent to this address may be featured on the Postcard Globe page at *www.postcardsfromhome.net*.

To include your postcard, include:
First name, City/Town, State/Region, and Country.
It will be used to post your postcard on the globe.

If you prefer your postcard not to be shared, please indicate that in your message.

*First Name:*__________
*City:*________ *State/Region* ______ *Country* ______

Send to:

Sandra Tarkleson
Postcards from H♥ME
PO Box 93
Malone, New York 12953

Personal Photos

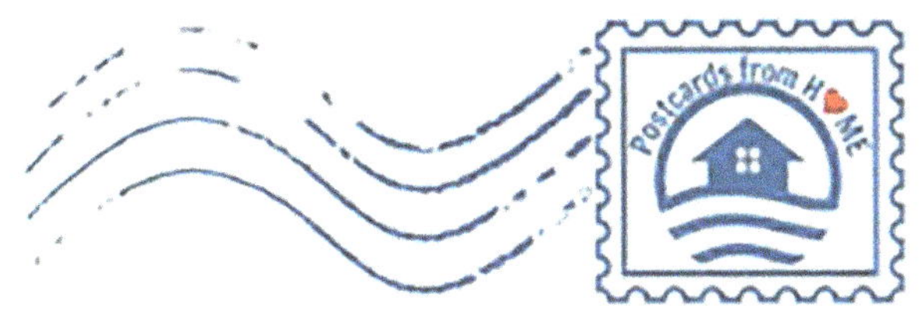

Tanner and I at my first Notre Dame football game.

Kallie and I after one of her many performances at Nazareth!

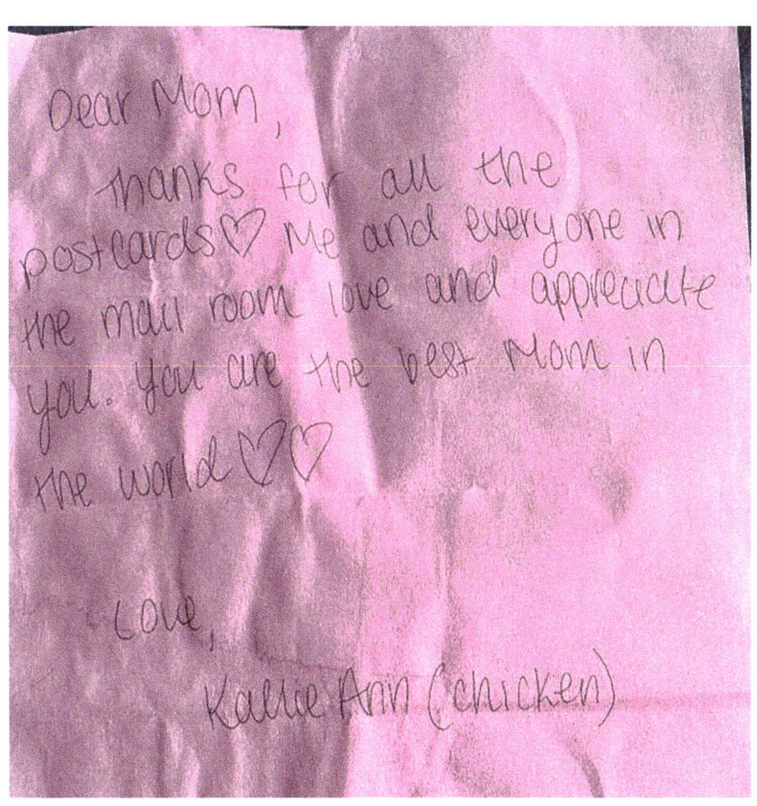

Dear Mom,
thanks for all the postcards♡ Me and everyone in the mail room love and appreciate you. You are the best Mom in the world♡♡

Love,
Kallie Ann (chicken)

Letter Kallie sent with encouragement from the Nazareth mailroom staff!

Kallie with Knute, and her wall of postcards sent to her

Tanner holding the gift to me of the first and last postcard sent to him while at Notre Dame.

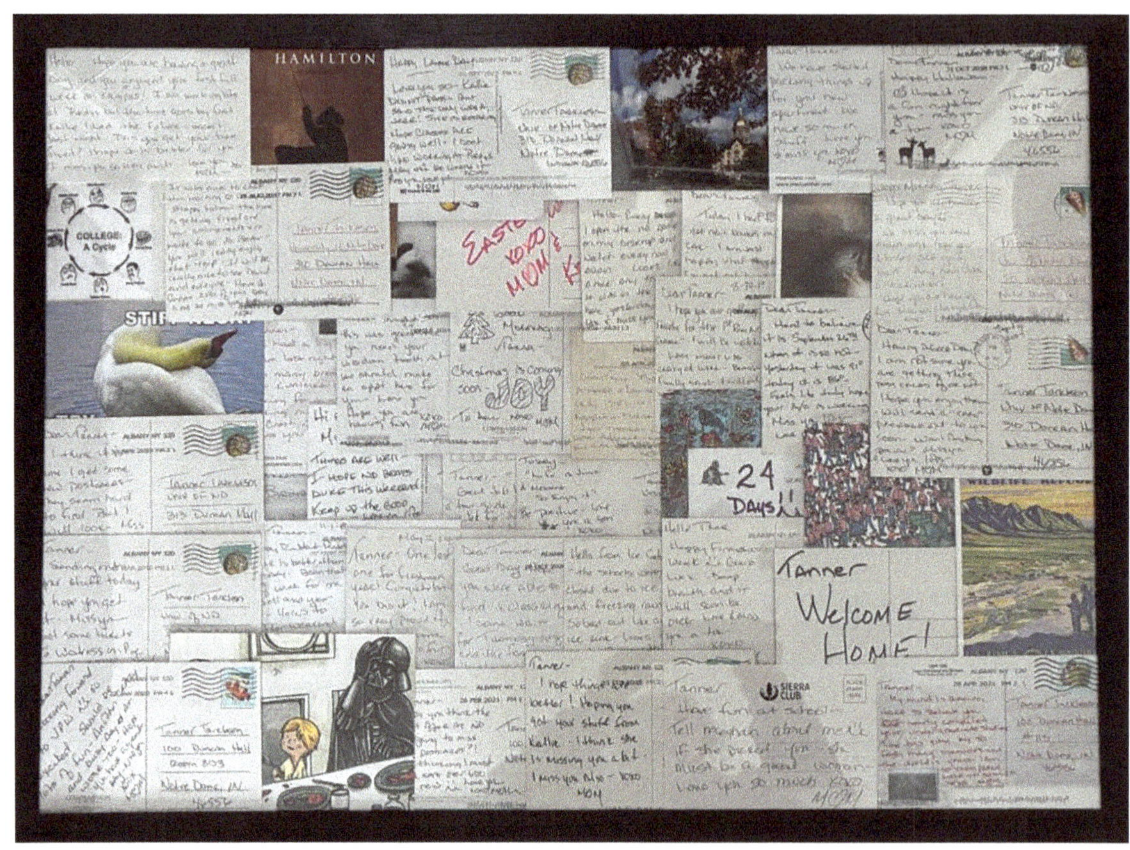
HAMILTON
COLLEGE: A Cycle
24 DAYS!!
Tanner
WELCOME HOME!
SIERRA CLUB

Some of the over 900 plus postcards they saved over the years.

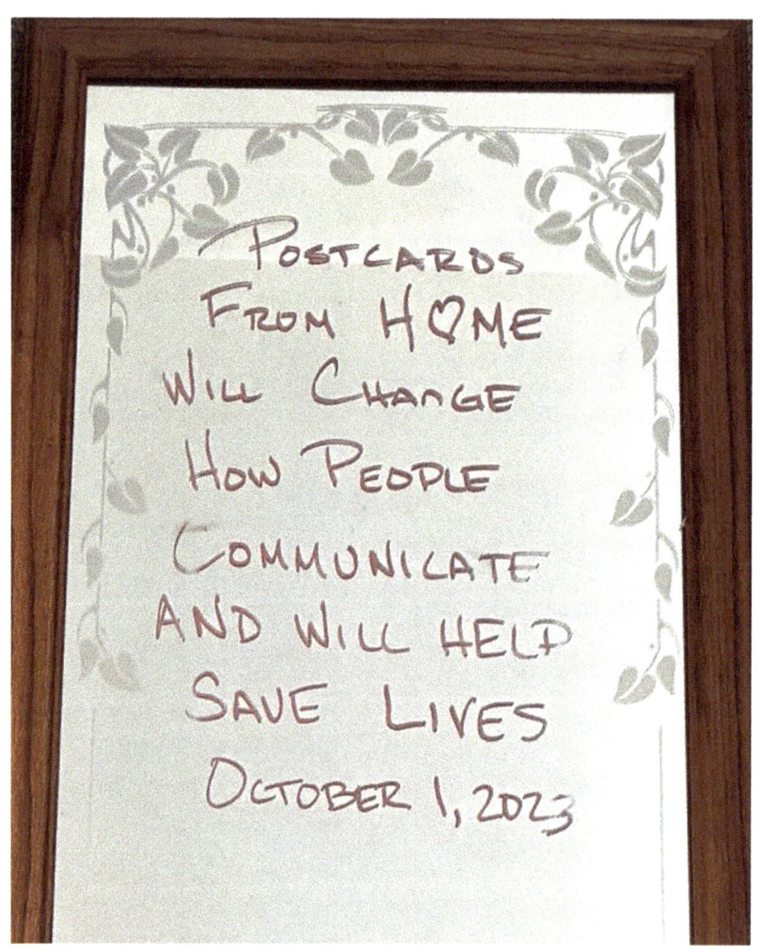

On October 1, 2023, I set the intention for this book, only to realize a few days later that it was International Postcard Day.

Acknowledgments

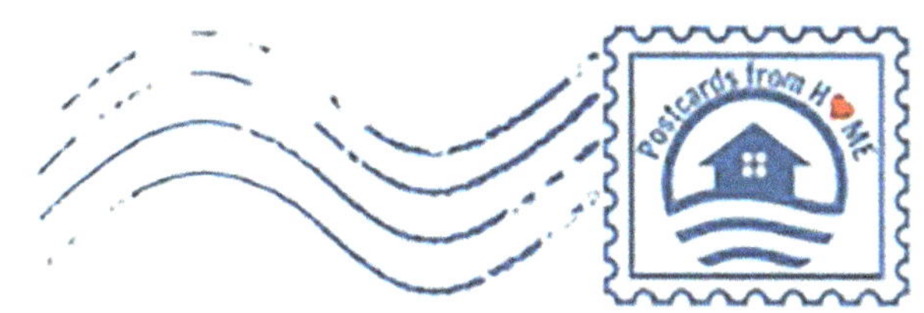

This book was written quietly, often in moments between responsibilities, reflection, and everyday life. It exists because of the people who showed up for me in ways both seen and unseen.

To my children, **Tanner** and **Kallie,** who I still see as five-year-olds, thank you for your patience, your resilience, and the love you bring into my life. Writing this book showed me how strong I have become, and it reminded me that when you love, there is nothing that is impossible. This book brought me back to myself. It made me cry, and it reminded me that through everything, love prevails.

To my **family** and **friends**, thank you for your steady presence, your encouragement, and your willingness to listen. Your support carried me through seasons when words felt heavy and uncertain.

To my editor, **Susan Crossman**, and my publisher, **Becky Norwood**, thank you for your thoughtful guidance, careful questions, and respect for the heart of this story. Your insight strengthened these pages and helped shape them into what they were meant to be.

And to every reader who has ever written a note, sent a card, or paused long enough to choose connection, thank you. Your words matter more than you may realize.

About the Author

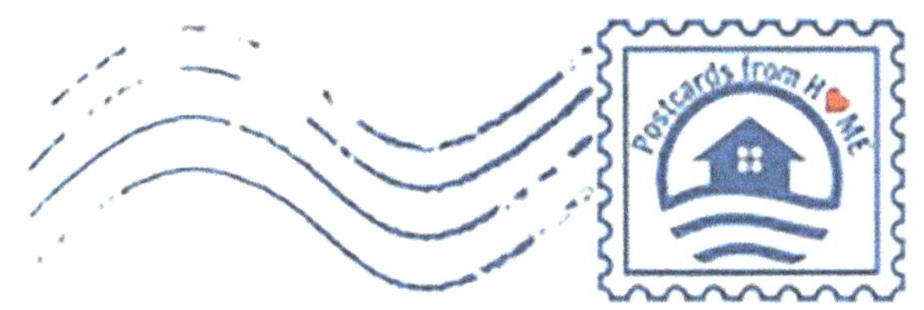

Sandra Tarkleson is the author of *Postcards from H♥ME*, a reflection on connection, presence, and the quiet power of handwritten words. Through seasons of change, transition, and rediscovery, she found meaning in the simple, intentional act of putting pen to paper and sending words out into the world.

What began as a personal practice became a way of staying connected across distance, time, and life's many chapters. Writing by hand offered a pause, a moment of honesty, and a reminder that even small acts of care can ripple farther than we imagine.

Sandra believes in presence, remaining open to change, and allowing herself to believe that there is purpose in all we do. She also believes that writing creates space for healing, reflection, and genuine human connection. When she is not writing, she can often be found walking her golden retriever, Knute, spending time with friends and family, and taking each day as the gift, it is.

www.ingramcontent.com/pod-product-compliance
Lightning Source LLC
Chambersburg PA
CBHW041036050726
47599CB00018B/1981
9781965761922